This is a singularly helpful book [...] ful series. It is helpful for three r[...] its thesis in Scripture, the courtes[...] who disagree, and the crisp clarity of the writing. Beyond these things is the importance of the subject. Books on this subject often become merely polemical, but this one is full of the majesty and grace of God.

—**D. A. Carson**, Trinity Evangelical Divinity School

Neither superficial nor highly technical, this new series of volumes on important Christian doctrines is projected to teach Reformed theology as it is most helpfully taught, with clear grounding in Scripture, mature understanding of theology, gracious interaction with others who disagree, and useful application to life. I expect that these volumes will strengthen the faith and biblical maturity of all who read them, and I am happy to recommend them highly.

—**Wayne Grudem**, Phoenix Seminary,
author of *Systematic Theology*

There are many misconceptions today about systematic, biblical, and applicatory theology. One sometimes gets the impression that these are opposed to one another, and that the first two, at least, are so obscure that ordinary people should avoid them like the plague. The series Explorations in Biblical Theology seeks to correct these misunderstandings, to bring these disciplines together in a winsome, clear unity, edifying to non-specialists. The authors are first-rate, and they write to build up our faith by pointing us to Christ. That's what biblical and systematic theology at their best have always done, and the best application of Scripture has always shown us in practical ways how to draw on the rich blessings of Jesus' salvation. I hope that many will read these books and take them to heart.

—**John Frame**, Reformed Theological Seminary

The message of a God who loved us before he formed the earth, called us his own before we could respond to him, died for us while we were dead in our transgressions and sins, made us alive when we were incapable of serving him, unites us to himself so that we can be forever holy, and now loves us more than we love ourselves—sparked a Reformation of hope and joy that transformed the world of faith. Re-declaring that hope and reclaiming that joy is the ambition and delight of this series. Able and godly scholars trace the golden thread of grace that unites all Scripture to make the wonders of our God's redeeming love shine and win hearts anew. The writing is warm, winsome, and respectful of those who differ. The motives are clearly to reveal truth and expose error by glorifying the message and manner of the Savior.

— **Bryan Chapell**, Covenant Theological Seminary

The aim of these volumes is clear: as regards God's Word, rigor; as regards other scholars, respect; as regards current issues, relevance; as regards the Lord himself, reverence. Effective witness and ministry currently require more than extra effort and better methods: the call is heard from churches across the board for renewal in our grasp of Christian truth. Each author in this series contributes admirably to that urgent need.

— **Robert W. Yarbrough**, Trinity Evangelical Divinity School

This is a series that the church needs more than ever, as we forge fresh links between the world of biblical studies and our Reformed theology. The contributors remind us again that the Bible is a book about God and his purposes and encourages us to preach and teach the message of salvation which it contains. It will be an inspiration to many and will give us new insight into the faith once delivered to the saints.

— **Gerald Bray**, Beeson Divinity School

The church of Jesus Christ faces massive cultural challenges today. More and more people in the Western world are ignorant of or hostile to the Christian faith. The moral fabric of our society is unraveling, and as a result of postmodernism many are adopting a relativistic worldview. Some Christians have responded by trying to simplify and dumb down the gospel. Others have tried to catch the cultural mood of the day in order to gain more converts, but they have often been co-opted by the culture instead of transforming it for Christ. What we truly need is to dig down deep into biblical foundations, so that our theology is robustly biblical. Only a worldview that is informed by both biblical and systematic theology can withstand the intellectual challenges that face us today. The series Explorations in Biblical Theology is designed to meet this very need. I commend these volumes enthusiastically, for they explain what the Scriptures teach from the standpoint of biblical theology. What we desperately need to hear and learn today is the whole counsel of God. This series advances that very agenda for the edification of the church and to the glory of God.

—**Thomas R. Schreiner**,
The Southern Baptist Theological Seminary

Explorations in Biblical Theology is a valuable new series of books on doctrinal themes that run through Scripture. The contributors are competent scholars who love to serve the church and have special expertise in the Bible and its theology. Following a thematic approach, each volume explores a distinctive doctrine as it is taught in Scripture, or else introduces the various doctrines taught in a particular book of the Bible. The result is a fresh and unique contribution to our understanding of the Bible's own theology.

—**Philip Ryken**, Tenth Presbyterian Church

Explorations in Biblical Theology is a gift to God's people. Biblical theology was never meant to be reserved for academics. When the verities of the Reformed faith are taken from the "ivy halls" of academia and placed in the hearts and minds of the covenant people of God, reformation and revival are the inevitable result. I believe God will use this series as a mighty tool for the Kingdom.

—**Steve Brown**, Reformed Theological Seminary

Election and
Free Will

Explorations in Biblical Theology

A Series

Robert A. Peterson, series editor

Election and Free Will

God's Gracious Choice and Our Responsibility

Robert A. Peterson

PUBLISHING
P.O. BOX 817 • PHILLIPSBURG • NEW JERSEY 08865-0817

Printed in the United States of America

Library of Congress Cataloging-in-Publication Data

Peterson, Robert A., 1948–
Election and free will : God's gracious choice and our responsibility /
Robert A. Peterson.
    p. cm.
Includes bibliographical references and indexes.
ISBN 978-0-87552-793-2 (pbk.)
1. Predestination. 2. Election (Theology). 3. Free will and determinism. I. Title.
BT810.3.P48 2007
234'.9—dc22
                        2007021790

With joy I dedicate this book to two groups of Covenant Theological Seminary students who studied election and free will with me in 2005:

to the Access class that met in July: David Bitler, David Chang, Alice Evans, David Marr, Christy Tayloe, and Gwen Westerlund

and to the fall evening class: Eleanor Brown, Norman Brown, Doug Hickel, Tricia Jackson, Karl Johnston, Henry Long, Matt Lybarger, Dayna Miller, and Libby Pruitt.

Contents

Series Introduction

Believers today need quality literature that attracts them to good theology and builds them up in their faith. Currently, readers may find several sets of lengthy—and rather technical—books on Reformed theology, as well as some that are helpful and semipopular. Explorations in Biblical Theology takes a more midrange approach, seeking to offer readers the substantial content of the more lengthy books, on the one hand, while striving for the readability of the semipopular books, on the other.

The series includes two types of books: (1) some treating biblical themes and (2) others treating the theology of specific biblical books. The volumes dealing with biblical themes seek to cover the whole range of Christian theology, from the doctrine of God to last things. Representative early offerings in the series focus on the empowering of the Holy Spirit, justification, the presence of God, preservation and apostasy, and substitutionary atonement. Examples of works dealing with the theology of specific biblical books include volumes on the theology of 1 and 2 Samuel, the Psalms, and Isaiah in the Old Testament, and books on the theology of Mark, Romans, and James in the New Testament.

Explorations in Biblical Theology is written for college seniors, seminarians, pastors, and thoughtful lay readers. These volumes are intended to be accessible and not obscured by excessive references to Hebrew, Greek, or theological jargon.

Each book seeks to be solidly Reformed in orientation, because the writers love the Reformed faith. The various theological themes and biblical books are treated from the perspective of biblical theology. Writers either trace doctrines through the

Bible or open up the theology of the specific books they treat. Writers desire not merely to dispense the Bible's good information, but also to apply that information to real needs today.

Explorations in Biblical Theology is committed to being warm and winsome, with a focus on applying God's truth to life. Authors aim to treat those with whom they disagree as they themselves would want to be treated. The motives for the rejection of error are not to fight, hurt, or wound, but to protect, help, and heal. The authors of this series will be godly, capable scholars with a commitment to Reformed theology and a burden to minister that theology clearly to God's people.

ROBERT A. PETERSON
Series Editor

Acknowledgments

I am grateful to friends who helped in the writing of this book:

Colleagues who read the manuscript and offered comments: David Calhoun, Jack Collins, Chris Morgan, Roger Price, Bob Pyne, Mark Ryan, Karen Sawyer, and Brian Vickers.

Matthew V. Novenson, my former teaching assistant, who wrote the last part of chapter 1 and most of chapter 2.

Wesley Vander Lugt, my current teaching assistant, who proofread and edited the entire manuscript.

Beth Ann Brown, Dana Ergenbright, and Rebecca Rine, who provided invaluable editorial assistance.

Librarians Steve Jamieson and James Pakala, who helped in research.

Angie Glassmeyer, Steve Lentz, Mary Pat Peterson, and David Richmon, readers who helped me achieve greater clarity.

Nick and Ellen Pappas, who graciously allowed me to spend many profitable days writing this book in their "farmhouse" in Bismarck, Missouri.

Why a Book on Election and Free Will?

In 1999, a theology professor wrote a book on election with the following dedication: "To all my students who for the past thirty-five years have asked more questions about this than any other topic."[1] Although I disagree with many of the conclusions of that professor, I heartily agree that the subject of election, or predestination (I will use the terms synonymously), raises many questions in people's minds. This book will try to answer many of those questions from the Scriptures. But first I must ask a basic question: why devote a book to the topic of predestination?

Today, we need a book dealing with biblical teaching on election and the related topic of free will for at least three good reasons:

- The Need for Graciousness in the Debate about Election
- The Tremendous Scriptural Witness to Election
- The Insecurity of Contemporary Life

The Need for Graciousness in the Debate about Election

There are two main positions among Christians concerning God's election of human beings for salvation: Arminianism and

1. Norman Geisler, *Chosen but Free: A Balanced View of Divine Election* (Minneapolis: Bethany House, 1999), 5.

1

Calvinism. Arminians believe that God in his sovereignty and grace chooses for salvation people whom he foresees will believe in Christ. By contrast, Calvinists hold that God in his sovereignty and grace chooses people for salvation without taking their responses into account; God chooses for reasons within himself. Unfortunately, Calvinists and Arminians have not always treated each other fairly, as quotations from the following two Web sites show.

Calvinist Ugliness

The first Web site is generated by a group of Calvinists seeking persons who agree with the following list of theological statements:

1. The gospel is the good news of salvation (including everything from regeneration to final glory) conditioned solely on the atoning blood and imputed righteousness of Christ.
2. Every regenerate person believes the gospel.
3. It is not possible for a regenerate person to confess a false gospel.
4. All Arminians (for the purposes of this list, an Arminian would be anyone who believes any or all of the following: partial depravity, conditional election, universal atonement, resistible grace, conditional perseverance) are unregenerate.
5. All who know what the doctrines of Arminianism are and believe that at least some Arminians are saved are unregenerate (this includes professing Calvinists who say that they remained Arminians for a time after they were regenerated or who say that some Arminians are their brothers in Christ).[2]

The Web site includes these words: "The few of us who believe the true gospel need to deepen our ties and encourage each other

2. Marc D. Carpenter, "From the Editor," in *Outside the Camp* 3.3 (1999), http://www.outsidethecamp.org/fte33.htm.

in the faith," and informs readers of plans to evangelize Arminians.[3] When I first read the words on this site, I hoped they were a bad joke. Sadly, however, the writers were very serious. As a Calvinist, I deplore the theological arrogance, religious bigotry, and lack of love evident in the above quotations.

Arminian Ugliness

Calvinists do not have a corner on the market when it comes to bad attitudes toward other Christians. Some Arminians return the favor, as these words from another Web site show:

> Five point Calvinists . . . typically bear fruit contrary to the teaching of God's Word. Specifically, it is typical of five point Calvinists to ignore or at times even oppose evangelism. After all, if all of humanity is either predestined to hell or to heaven, and there is nothing anyone can do to switch from one group to the other regardless of their will, then why evangelize? The elect will be saved whether they like it or not, and the non-elect will be doomed whether they want to or not. . . . Five point Calvinists tend to speak of love and grace frequently, but display very little of either. Rather than loving and serving the lost and hurting, they are engaged in continual arguing, often dividing the Body of Christ in a legalistic and hurtful manner. . . .
>
> Such a belief makes God a monster who eternally tortures innocent children, it removes the hope of consolation from the Gospel, it limits the atoning work of Christ, it resists evangelism, it stirs up argumentation and division, and it promotes a small, angry, judgmental God rather than the large-hearted God of the Bible.[4]

Ironically, although the Web site just quoted blames Calvinists for bad theology and bad fruit, the gross generalizations, misrepresentations, and absence of love evident in the quotation represent neither good theology nor good fruit.

3. Ibid.
4. Larry Taylor, *Calvinism vs. Arminianism: A Discussion of Doctrine*, Calvary Chapel Cheyenne, http://www3.calvarychapel.com/cheyenne/Books/CVAFrCal.html.

An Attempt to Do Better

Admittedly, I have chosen extreme examples of unfairness and intolerance on both sides. Most interaction between the two camps is not as extreme, but still is lacking in courtesy. An example is found in the writings of Norman Geisler and James R. White on the topic of election. In 1999, Geisler wrote *Chosen but Free*, a book on election in which he, among other things, strongly opposed traditional Calvinism. James White was agitated by Geisler's book and wrote a reply titled *The Potter's Freedom: A Defense of the Reformation and a Rebuttal of Norman Geisler's* Chosen but Free.[5] White's book in turn prompted Geisler, in a second edition of his work, to add an appendix, "A Response to James White's *The Potter's Freedom*."[6]

Although these men are generally courteous toward one another, they are not above emotive language and even name-calling in presenting each other's positions. For example, the Calvinist White, offended by Geisler's characterization of Calvinism, strings together several of Geisler's most inflammatory anti-Calvinist comments in a rhetorically loaded opening salvo:

> This system [Calvinism] seems particularly pernicious in Dr. Geisler's view. . . . It can "have a devastating effect on one's own salvation, to say nothing of one's enthusiasm to reach others for Christ." This belief even lays the ground for universalism, undermines trust in the love of God, and in so doing has even been the "occasion for disbelief and even atheism for many." The God presented by adherents of this system "is not worthy of worship" and "does not represent God at all. . . ." This system is at its heart "theologically inconsistent, philosophically insufficient, and morally repugnant."[7]

5. James R. White, *The Potter's Freedom: A Defense of the Reformation and a Rebuttal of Norman Geisler's* Chosen but Free (Amityville, NY: Calvary Press, 2000).

6. Norman Geisler, *Chosen but Free: A Balanced View of Divine Election*, 2nd ed. (Minneapolis: Bethany House, 2001), 252–63.

7. White, *The Potter's Freedom*, 17–18.

But if White is irritated at his opponent, Geisler is certainly no less so. Indeed, in the second edition of his book he devotes a lengthy appendix to the sole purpose of rebutting White in equally provocative language (using the abbreviation *PF* for White's *The Potter's Freedom*):

> Sometimes my view is so distorted by stereotype that it seems almost impossible to believe that *PF* had my book in mind . . .
> *I counted no less than forty times my view was misrepresented* . . . This failure to comprehend my position does not impede in the least the overly zealous, pedantic, and at times somewhat arrogant critique of it in *PF* . . .
> *PF*'s favorite name-calling device is what its author believes is the theologically toxic word, "Arminian" . . .
> I am not alone in detecting a proud and exclusivistic undertone in *PF* . . .
> *By distorting the obvious, caricaturing the opposing, and sidestepping the difficult, PF futilely attempts to make the implausible sound plausible and the unbiblical seem biblical.*[8]

Too often, the debate between Calvinists and Arminians has failed to glorify God, promote understanding, or foster honor for one another as fellow members of the body of Christ. I could easily multiply examples, but will refrain in a desire to edify. I aim, however, to treat my Arminian brothers and sisters in Christ as I would want to be treated. Toward that end, I will use the best sources for Arminian theology, will acknowledge the truths that we share in common as evangelical Christians, and will endeavor to appreciate the valid concerns of Arminian Christians. Nevertheless, I am a Calvinist and, while admitting that no theology has all the answers and that my position has weaknesses, will make the best case for Calvinism that I can. That case begins by demonstrating how much the Bible says about election or predestination.

8. Geisler, *Chosen but Free*, 2nd ed., 254, 256, 262–63 (italics in original).

The Tremendous Scriptural Witness to Election

A second reason why a book on election and free will is needed today is that many Christians are unaware of the tremendous number of scriptural passages that speak of God's electing people. As a result, many have neglected a significant biblical theme. I will quote a sampling of passages (and list many others) dealing with the election of Israel, Christ, and the church.

God's Election of Israel

Numerous passages speak of God's choosing Israel alone, out of all the nations on the earth, to belong to him.

> He loved your fathers and chose their offspring after them and brought you out of Egypt with his own presence, by his great power, driving out before you nations greater and mightier than yourselves, to bring you in, to give you their land for an inheritance, as it is this day. (Deut. 4:37–38)

> For you are a people holy to the LORD your God. The LORD your God has chosen you to be a people for his treasured possession, out of all the peoples who are on the face of the earth. It was not because you were more in number than any other people that the LORD set his love on you and chose you, for you were the fewest of all peoples, but it is because the LORD loves you and is keeping the oath that he swore to your fathers, that the LORD has brought you out with a mighty hand and redeemed you from the house of slavery, from the hand of Pharaoh king of Egypt. (Deut. 7:6–8)

> Behold, to the LORD your God belong heaven and the heaven of heavens, the earth with all that is in it. Yet the LORD set his heart in love on your fathers and chose their offspring after them, you above all peoples, as you are this day. (Deut. 10:14–15)

> Blessed is the nation whose God is the LORD,
> the people whom he has chosen as his heritage! (Ps. 33:12)

6

But you, Israel, my servant,
   Jacob, whom I have chosen,
   the offspring of Abraham, my friend;
you whom I took from the ends of the earth,
   and called from its farthest corners,
saying to you, "You are my servant,
   I have chosen you and not cast you off";
fear not, for I am with you;
   be not dismayed, for I am your God;
I will strengthen you, I will help you,
   I will uphold you with my righteous right hand. (Isa. 41:8–10)

Many other passages also deal with the election of Israel, including Deuteronomy 14:2; 1 Kings 3:8; 1 Chronicles 16:13; Psalms 105:6, 43; 106:5; 135:4; Isaiah 44:1–2; 45:4; Acts 13:17; and Romans 11:28–29.

God's Election of the Messiah

Although the majority of the election passages in Scripture concern God's choice of Israel and his choice of the church, a few passages speak of God's choosing the Messiah.

Behold my servant, whom I uphold,
   my chosen, in whom my soul delights;
I have put my Spirit upon him;
   he will bring forth justice to the nations. (Isa. 42:1)

Behold, my servant whom I have chosen,
   my beloved with whom my soul is well pleased. (Matt. 12:18)

And a voice came out of the cloud, saying, "This is my Son, my Chosen One; listen to him!" (Luke 9:35)

And the people stood by, watching, but the rulers scoffed at him, saying, "He saved others; let him save himself, if he is the Christ of God, his Chosen One!" (Luke 23:35)

7

He was foreknown before the foundation of the world . . . , a living stone rejected by men but in the sight of God chosen and precious. (1 Peter 1:20; 2:4)

God's Election of the Church

An abundance of passages from all parts of the New Testament tell of God's election of individuals and of the Christian church. I will quote ten and list almost three times that many.

And if those days had not been cut short, no human being would be saved. But for the sake of the elect those days will be cut short. (Matt. 24:22)

I am praying for them. I am not praying for the world but for those whom you have given me, for they are yours. (John 17:9)

And when the Gentiles heard this, they began rejoicing and glorifying the word of the Lord, and as many as were appointed to eternal life believed. (Acts 13:48)

For those whom he foreknew he also predestined to be conformed to the image of his Son, in order that he might be the firstborn among many brothers. And those whom he predestined he also called, and those whom he called he also justified, and those whom he justified he also glorified. (Rom. 8:29–30)

What if God, desiring to show his wrath and to make known his power, has endured with much patience vessels of wrath prepared for destruction, in order to make known the riches of his glory for vessels of mercy, which he has prepared beforehand for glory? (Rom. 9:22–23)

He chose us in him before the foundation of the world, that we should be holy and blameless before him. In love he predestined us for adoption through Jesus Christ, according to the purpose of his will, to the praise of his glorious grace, with which he has blessed us in the Beloved. (Eph. 1:4–6)

In him we have obtained an inheritance, having been predestined according to the purpose of him who works all things according to the counsel of his will, so that we who were the first to hope in Christ might be to the praise of his glory. (Eph. 1:11–12)

[God] saved us and called us to a holy calling, not because of our works but because of his own purpose and grace, which he gave us in Christ Jesus before the ages began. (2 Tim. 1:9)

Therefore, brothers, be all the more diligent to make your calling and election sure, for if you practice these qualities you will never fall. (2 Peter 1:10)

And the dwellers on earth whose names have not been written in the book of life from the foundation of the world will marvel to see the beast. (Rev. 17:8b)

Other predestination passages in the New Testament: Matthew 22:14; 24:24, 31; Mark 13:20, 22, 27; Luke 18:7; John 6:37; 13:18; 15:16, 19; 17:2, 6, 24; Acts 18:9–10; Romans 8:33; 9:10–13; 11:5, 7; Colossians 3:12; 1 Thessalonians 1:4; 2 Thessalonians 2:13; 2 Timothy 2:10; Titus 1:1; James 2:5; 1 Peter 1:1–2; 2:9; 5:13; and Revelation 17:14.

If nothing else, the sheer volume of biblical data on divine choosing, electing, and predestinating demands that we give thoughtful attention to the subject. Unfortunately, throughout the long history of this doctrine, some have paid it too little attention (thereby missing an important biblical point), and others too much (thereby distorting other parts of their theology). Our goal is to give election the amount and type of attention that Scripture itself does. We will take care to note the ways in which predestination relates to other biblical truths and the ways in which the Scriptures use the doctrine of predestination.

The Insecurity of Contemporary Life[9]

A third reason why Christians need to read a book on election and free will is the insecurity of much of contemporary life. Ironically, although the doctrine of election has sometimes been accused of unsettling people, within the Bible its function is largely to comfort the people of God and assure them that underneath all their meager efforts to live for him are God's everlasting arms to hold, protect, and caress them. This is as important today as ever because of the many reasons why people feel insecure.

Dysfunctional Families

One need not look far for examples of family dysfunction; most of us can point to instances in our own families. I think of one student at our seminary whose father left when he was a young boy and who was then raised by his alcoholic single mom. Now barely into his twenties, he and his wife of three years are in the awkward position of looking after his chronically unstable mother. When she comes to stay with them, they have to hide whatever alcohol and money there may be in the house to eliminate any possibility of further dissipation on her part. The young seminary couple is quite willing to help out in this way, but their pain is understandably great.

I also think of a young woman in our church who was raised by her mentally ill mother after the father left the family. By God's grace, the young woman made it to college, where she met and married a Christian man. About the same time, however, her mother was institutionalized by the state, leaving behind a five-year-old daughter (my friend's younger sister) on the street. When it became clear that the little girl's only options were homelessness or foster care, the new bride undertook to adopt her own younger sister. Thankfully, the adoption has gone through, which was the best possible outcome given the situa-

9. I am pleased to acknowledge Matthew V. Novenson, my former teaching assistant, for providing considerable help in writing the remainder of this chapter.

tion. But even so, the difficult process left the mother furious, the little girl emotionally scarred, and the newlywed couple spread very thin.

And these unhappy cases are not atypical. Less than a quarter of my evangelical Christian friends have avoided the pain of divorce among their relatives. My purpose is not to add to the guilt of divorced persons but to point to the heavy toll that divorce is taking on today's families. The former certainties of solid extended families living in the same town are distant memories for many. In such a situation, we must ask: are there aspects of God's truth, including election, that can help mend broken hearts?

Technological Loneliness

A friend named Susan recently took an overseas flight on a major international airline. Because it had been a number of years since she had flown that far, one feature of the flight took her by surprise. She had expected to hear the usual chatter between seatmates all over the plane, perhaps even to get to know the person in the seat next to her. You can imagine Susan's surprise, then, when as soon as they were in the air, all the people on the plane were sitting silent, headphones on, eyes fixed on the small screen in the back of the seat in front of them. On that eight-hour flight, she heard scarcely a word exchanged between passengers. With their private movie screens and headphones, they were entertained, yes, but at the expense of any significant human interaction.

The airplane story is a mundane example of a phenomenon that is widespread in our day—technological loneliness. True, technology adds all sorts of wonderful conveniences to our lives, but the very machines that have made modern life so much easier have made it harder for us to spend meaningful time with other people. Computers have changed the way we live for the better but have also brought new problems into our lives. Wives fight to save their marriages to husbands who are addicted to computer pornography. Some people become so enamored of the latest technological gadgets that their personal relationships suffer. We are more adept at controlling our world than our forebears were, but have we sacrificed intimacy for technological wizardry? In an impersonal technological culture, might the message of God's personal control over people's lives meet a deeply felt need in their hearts?

Fear of Terrorism

A thirty-something-year-old woman in St. Louis, living the homosexual lifestyle and simultaneously dabbling in religion, was deeply disturbed by the news that hijackers had crashed planes into the World Trade Center buildings on September 11, 2001. For days after the attack, she was plagued by feelings of overwhelming fear and uncertainty. She found herself unable to concentrate on even the most routine of daily tasks.

During this time, the woman happened to be browsing one day in a sidewalk bookstore when she came upon a popular Christian book on biblical prophecy. Much of the book was incomprehensible to her, but the basic idea of a God who held the future safely in his powerful hands affected her profoundly. She could not seem to get the idea out of her head. It was just the sort of thing she had been longing to hear, and now here was a book saying that it was not just wishful thinking, but in fact the very truth about the universe.

That paperback set off a remarkable chain of events in the woman's life. Intrigued by the author's vision of a God who is sovereign over the affairs of the world, she searched the Internet for the author's name and church affiliation. This led her to an evangelical ministry for people in the homosexual lifestyle. That ministry referred the woman to an evangelical church in St. Louis, a church that taught the same doctrine of divine sovereignty that had first caught her attention in the sidewalk bookstore. At that church she heard the gospel, came to saving faith in Christ, and came to know the God who holds the future in his hands.

Greater airport security increases our sense of safety but at the same time reminds us of the terrorist attacks of 9/11. When the towers collapsed, a friend of mine lost six men whom he was discipling. Our world has been changed by 9/11; new fears have been introduced into American life. Does God's Word concerning his control of all things, including salvation, speak to such fears?

Radical Autonomy

Richard Bauckham, in his perceptive book *God and the Crisis of Freedom*, sums up the false notion of freedom that is dominant in the West:

> In its sublimest form the modern myth of humanity's godlike freedom . . . forms the background to virtually all concrete thinking about freedom. It means that freedom is felt to be opposed to all limits. Freedom means the ability to determine oneself however one wishes by making any choices without restriction. In contemporary Britain this kind of freedom is thought to be available in two major forms: freedom of opportunity and freedom of consumer choice.[10]

In describing Great Britain, Bauckham also describes America and the rest of the Western world. Many regard true freedom as freedom to choose their work and lifestyle and freedom to buy more and more of what they want. For many, however, the endless pursuit of such autonomy has resulted in increasing dissatisfaction. The more we acquire, the more we become aware of the emptiness of modern life. How does the modern notion of radical autonomy square with Scripture? What does God say about true freedom? How does true freedom relate to God's sovereign control and election?

In short, contemporary life is characterized by much insecurity in a variety of spheres. We have only briefly discussed

10. Richard Bauckham, *God and the Crisis of Freedom: Biblical and Contemporary Perspectives* (Louisville: Westminster John Knox Press, 2002), 33–34.

family dysfunction, technological loneliness, fear of terrorism, and radical autonomy. These are some of the most obvious and most important forms of modern insecurity, but by no means do they exhaust the list. This generation is well acquainted with the feeling that the world is lurching out of control, and it is therefore also well suited for the biblical message about a God who sovereignly works all things for the good of his people.

Conclusion

There is a real need, then, for a fresh look at the Bible's teaching concerning election and free will for at least three reasons. First, Calvinists and Arminians have frequently not debated the issues fairly and respectfully. Second, to the surprise of some, a great many scriptural texts treat the subject of election. To shun the topic of election, therefore, is to ignore much of the Bible. And third, many factors have produced insecurity in contemporary life. If we will only listen, God's Word offers great confidence and comfort when it reveals the purposes of predestination and the makeup of true freedom.

A road map is in order: After surveying the ideas of key figures in church history about election (chapter 2), we will explore what the various parts of the Bible say (chapters 3 to 7). Next we will consider the vital topic of free will (chapter 8). We will conclude by telling the Bible's story of predestination and underscoring the ways in which God wants the message of election to affect our lives (chapters 9 and 10).

Election and Free Will
in Church History

"There are two things about the doctrine of predestination that cannot be gainsaid: it is important, and it is controversial."[1]

The church's story of election and free will bears out this quotation by Paul Jewett, as the relation between divine control and human freedom has been a perennial issue. There is no one historical position on the question of predestination and free will. It would be misleading, then, to say that the story of Christian theology is only a story of monergism, the view that salvation is ultimately attributable only to God, as Calvinists have sometimes claimed. But it is equally wrong to say that the story of Christian theology is only a story of synergism, the view that salvation is ultimately attributable to both God and human beings working together, as Arminians have sometimes claimed. Rather, both strands go far back and persist in the Christian tradition.

So many figures in church history have written on election that an exhaustive survey of their writings is beyond this book's scope. But we will survey the most important episodes in the history of this doctrine. Our goal is to gain background for our investigation of Scripture in the next five chapters.

I thank Matthew V. Novenson, my former teaching assistant, for his outstanding work in researching and substantially writing this chapter.

1. Paul Jewett, *Election and Predestination* (Grand Rapids: Eerdmans, 1985), 1.

- The Ancient Period (AD 1–500)
  - The Early Church Fathers
  - Augustine (354–430) and Pelagius (354–435)
- The Medieval Period (AD 500–1500)
  - Semi-Pelagianism
  - The Synod of Orange (529)
  - Thomas Aquinas (ca. 1225–74)
- The Reformation Period (AD 1500–1700)
  - Martin Luther (1483–1546) and Desiderius Erasmus (1466–1536)
  - John Calvin (1509–64)
  - Jacob Arminius (1560–1609)
  - The Synod of Dort (1618–19)
- The Modern Period (AD 1700–Present)
  - The Enlightenment
  - John Wesley (1703–91) and George Whitefield (1714–70)
  - Charles Finney (1792–1875)
  - Charles Haddon Spurgeon (1834–92) and the "Hyperists"
  - Friedrich Schleiermacher (1768–1834)
  - Karl Barth (1886–1968)
  - Today

The Ancient Period (AD 1-500)

The Early Church Fathers

Aside from the Scriptures, our earliest sources for the doctrines of election and free will are the apostolic fathers, the first generation of church leaders after the apostles. There is little of the doctrine of grace in the apostolic fathers, as Thomas Torrance famously concluded.[2] One excerpt from *The Shepherd of*

2. Thomas Torrance, *The Doctrine of Grace in the Apostolic Fathers* (Grand Rapids: Eerdmans, 1959).

Hermas illustrates: "Believe in [God], therefore, and fear him, and fearing him, be self-controlled. Keep these things, and you will cast off all evil from yourself and will put on every virtue of righteousness and will live to God, if you keep this command-ment."[3] This theme of earnest moralism is characteristic of the apostolic fathers. Moralism is the making of performance—rather than grace—the standard or norm for acceptance.

The fathers of the third and fourth centuries expanded on their basic continuity with the apostolic fathers by outlining a robust doc-trine of free will. On the relation between salvation and the human will, Clement of Alexandria (ca. 220) commented, "Nor shall he who is saved be saved against his will. . . . God ministers salvation to those who cooperate for the attainment of knowledge and good conduct."[4] John Chrysostom (ca. 400), the great preacher of Constantinople, insisted on the inviolability of the human will: "All depends indeed on God, but not so that our free will is hindered . . . [God] does not anticipate our choice, lest our free will should be outraged. But when we have chosen, then great is the assistance he brings to us."[5] These statements represent progress from the simpler moralism of the apostolic fathers, but they agree with them in their earnest piety and in the absence of a doctrine of electing grace.

Augustine (354–430) and Pelagius (354–435)

Although controversy over predestination has recurred regu-larly in the history of the church, there are two great peaks in the mountain range, two periods that set the terms for all subsequent discussion. The second of these, the controversy surrounding Jacob Arminius, will be discussed below. But the first and greater

3. *The Shepherd of Hermas* 2.1, in *The Ante-Nicene Fathers*, ed. Alexander Donaldson and James Donaldson, vol. 1 (Grand Rapids: Eerdmans, 1951), 20; I credit Roger Olson (The Story of Christian Theology [Downer's Grove, IL: Intervarsity Press, 1999], 51) for pointing out this reference.

4. Quoted in H. Orton Wiley, *Christian Theology*, 3 vols. (Kansas City, MO: Beacon Hill Press, 1940–43), 2:347.

5. John Chrysostom, *Homilies on Hebrews*, in *Nicene and Post-Nicene Fathers*, ed. Philip Schaff, vol. 14 1st ser. (Grand Rapids: Eerdmans, 1979), 425; David Calhoun pointed me to this reference.

peak was the dispute between the North African bishop Augustine and the British moralist Pelagius.

Born in 354 to a Christian mother and a pagan father in Thagaste, North Africa, the young Augustine pursued the worldly pleasures available to a young man of status in the late Roman Empire. As a young professor of rhetoric with a taste for philosophy, he immersed himself first in Manichaeanism and then in Neoplatonism. He became interested in Christianity while studying the rhetoric of the sermons of Ambrose, bishop of Milan.

Under Ambrose's influence, Augustine studied Paul's epistles and became overwhelmed with the gravity of his guilt before God. While pleading with the Lord for deliverance, he came to Romans 13:13–14: "Let us walk properly as in the daytime, not in orgies and drunkenness, not in sexual immorality and sensuality, not in quarreling and jealousy. But put on the Lord Jesus Christ, and make no provision for the flesh, to gratify its desires." Then, Augustine writes in his *Confessions*, "As the sentence ended—by a light, as it were, of security infused into my heart—all the gloom of doubt vanished away."[6]

The newly converted Augustine returned to his native North Africa, where he later came to be appointed the bishop of Hippo. From there he began to write, and his popularity grew. Through Augustine's influence, the idea of divine monergism gained wide acceptance not only in Hippo but also as far as Rome itself, which provided occasion for controversy when Pelagius came there in 405.

Pelagius, born in Britain in 354, was interested in monasticism and made a name for himself as an advocate of Christian moralism. He was appointed to a teaching post in Rome, where he arrived in 405 to a city heavy with its own vice. Here was the capital of the Christian empire, in a state of moral degradation! And why? Pelagius heard Christians in Rome approvingly repeating the prayer from Augustine's *Confessions*: "Grant what

6. Augustine, *Confessions* 8.29, in *Nicene and Post-Nicene Fathers*, vol. 1 1st ser., 130.

you command, and command what you will."[7] Pelagius, putting two and two together, concluded that Augustine's view of grace led inevitably to sin. He opposed it out of a concern for proper Christian ethics.

For his part, Augustine's view of sin and grace was tied to his conversion experience. So great was his sense of his own sinfulness, and of the divine mercy necessary to deliver him from it, that he formulated a doctrine of grace in which salvation is all of God, with no human will or effort. This doctrine of grace appears early in autobiographical form in the *Confessions* and later in more systematic form in the several anti-Pelagian writings.[8]

On the matter of free will, about which Augustine was criticized in his own day and has been ever since, he understood human freedom to be simply the ability to do what one wills. If, in any given case, we can act as we will to act, then we are free in that case. The complication is that since Adam's fall, human free will is in bondage to sin.[9] We still have "natural freedom," insofar as we can still do as we will. But because of original sin, the will itself is now bent toward sin, so that we inevitably will to sin and act sinfully.

In this disastrous situation, if salvation is to come to us at all, it can be only as a free gift of divine grace. Grace does not simply provide the option of salvation; it always accomplishes what it purposes. On this Augustinian understanding, *prevenient grace* (grace that "comes before") has an important place. And this prevenient grace is particular and effective, rather than general and potential.[10]

If this is true, then why do some people receive God's grace and others not? Augustine answered: "The reason why one person

7. Augustine, *Confessions*, trans. Henry Chadwick (Oxford: Oxford University Press, 1991), 202.

8. These are, in chronological order: *On the Spirit and the Letter* (412); *On Nature and Grace* (415); *On the Grace of Christ and Original Sin* (418); *On Grace and Free Will* (427); and *On the Predestination of the Saints* (429).

9. Augustine, *The Enchiridion* 30–32, in *Nicene and Post-Nicene Fathers*, vol. 3 1st ser., 247–48.

10. Augustine, *On Predestination* 10.19, in *Nicene and Post-Nicene Fathers*, vol. 5 1st ser., 507.

is assisted by grace and another is not helped must be referred to the secret judgments of God."[11] For Augustine, the principle of discrimination lies in God, not in us, and human beings should not speculate regarding God's reasons.

For the moralist Pelagius, the idea that *moral responsibility* entails *moral ability* was a first principle. If God holds us responsible to act in a certain way, he reasoned, it must be within our power to act in that way. If not, God would be unjust in holding us responsible. So Pelagius rejected Augustine's doctrine of original sin, the idea that Adam's guilt and corruption were passed on to all subsequent human beings. Adam's sin affects us only insofar as he set us a poor example to follow.

In Pelagius's view, every person is free at every moment to choose either good or evil. Nothing inclines us toward one or the other. Grace, then, is not a divine renewal of the will or even divine moral assistance. Rather, grace is the revelation of God's moral will—first in creation, then in the Mosaic Law, and finally in Jesus' life.

The theologies of Augustine and Pelagius collided. The controversy between the two men carried over the better part of two decades. Both had their supporters, but the courts of the church judged decisively against the views of Pelagius. Pelagianism was condemned at the ecumenical Council of Ephesus (431).

With regard to subsequent developments, nearly as important as the positions themselves are the reasons why Augustine and Pelagius believed as they did. Augustine's troubled conscience and vision of God's incomparable power led him to oppose any credit of merit to the human will. Pelagius's concern for Christian holiness drove him to challenge what he saw as license on Augustine's part. This is important because not only the positions but also the reasons for holding them were inherited by generations of followers on both sides.

11. Augustine, *On Grace and Free Will* 23.45, in *Nicene and Post-Nicene Fathers*, vol. 5 1st ser., 464.

The Medieval Period (AD 500–1500)

Semi-Pelagianism

For all their differences, the one thing that Augustinianism and Pelagianism had in common was that both were monergisms—Augustinianism a divine monergism (grace alone) and Pelagianism a human monergism (merit alone). But in the generation after the two men, both monergisms gave way (Pelagianism by official condemnation, Augustinianism by theological development) to a new synergism. This was actually a revival of the moralism of the earlier fathers, and it came to be called "semi-Pelagianism."

The semi-Pelagians followed Pelagius in rejecting Augustine's doctrine of the bondage of the will, but they stopped short of affirming Pelagius's doctrine of absolute free will. Instead, they developed a doctrine of "weakened free will." On this understanding, people initiate grace, and God rewards them with divine aid. In the words of John Cassian, "When [God] sees in us some beginnings of a good will, he at once enlightens it and strengthens it and urges it on toward salvation."[12]

The Synod of Orange (529)

The next major ecclesiastical event in the story was the Synod of Orange (529). Here the condemnation of Pelagianism was reaffirmed. But more importantly, Augustinian sympathizers won the day as semi-Pelagianism was also condemned. Yet the synod stopped short of affirming Augustine's full-fledged doctrine of predestination. The synod affirmed Augustine's doctrines of original sin and moral inability; but in a silence that spoke volumes, the synod did not mention election to salvation. What emerged at Orange, then, was something new—neither Augustinianism nor Pelagianism, nor even semi-Pelagianism, but what has properly

12. John Cassian, *Third Conference of Abbot Chaeremon* 8, in *Nicene and Post-Nicene Fathers*, vol. 11 2nd ser., 426.

been called "semi-Augustinianism." This is a synergism in which God initiates grace, but people must cooperate via free will.

Thomas Aquinas (ca. 1225–74)

Not every teacher of the church agreed with this view of things. On the contrary, Thomas Aquinas, the most important figure in all of medieval theology, was convinced of Augustine's view of predestination. Whereas Augustine had located election in the doctrine of salvation, Thomas located it in the doctrine of general providence: "It is fitting that God should predestine men, for all things are subject to his providence."[13] But despite his differences in method, in substance the monergism of Thomas was virtually indistinguishable from that of Augustine, as is evident from another statement of Thomas: "Grace works in its own power." The official church doctrine was a gracious synergism, but almost as influential was the monergism of Thomas.

Thomas was not the only voice in the medieval church for Augustine's view of election. Centuries before him had been Bede, Alcuin, and Isidore of Seville. In the ninth century, Gottschalk, a Benedictine brother, revived the Augustinian view of sin and grace. He was theologically opposed by Rabanus Maurus and ecclesiastically opposed by Bishop Hincmar of Rheims. In the end, the unfortunate monk was convicted of heresy and imprisoned until his death twenty years later. In the later Middle Ages, Thomas Bradwardine, Gregory of Rimini, and John Wycliffe represented a resurgence of Augustinian predestination among theologians.

The Reformation Period (AD 1500–1700)

The Protestant view of predestination has come to be known as Calvinism, but in fact all three major Reformers (Martin Luther,

13. Thomas Aquinas, *Summa Theologica* 1a.23.1, Blackfriars ed. (New York: McGraw-Hill, 1963).

Ulrich Zwingli, and John Calvin) followed the view of predestination taught by Augustine and Thomas. The Reformation itself started with Luther, and fittingly, so too did the Reformation-era discussion of election and free will. The occasion was a debate between Luther and the great Dutch humanist Desiderius Erasmus of Rotterdam.

Martin Luther (1483–1546) and Desiderius Erasmus (1466–1536)

Luther was an Augustinian friar, a Bible professor, and (increasingly from 1517 onward) an inflammatory German Reformer. Luther understood the doctrines of election and the bondage of the will to highlight the absolute graciousness of God, especially in justification. So when Erasmus published his *On the Freedom of the Will* in 1524, Luther congratulated him for getting right to the heart of the burning issue of the day, the question of monergism versus synergism: what, if anything, do human beings contribute to the process of divine grace?

Concerning free will, Erasmus took up the mantle of the sixth-century semi-Pelagians, arguing for a weakened free will: "For although free choice is damaged by sin, it is nevertheless not extinguished by it. And although it has become so lame in the process that before we receive grace we are more readily inclined toward evil than good, yet it is not altogether cut out . . ."[14] This sounded to Luther dangerously like Pelagianism. Erasmus dodged such accusations by affirming the necessity of God's cooperating grace.

Luther responded to Erasmus by writing a book, the title of which was a rebuke to Erasmus. In *On the Bondage of the Will*, Luther agrees that there is such a thing as absolute free will, but insists that only God has it. Following Augustine's doctrine of original sin, Luther argues that since the fall the human will has been enslaved to sin. But Luther's most enduring contribution to the discussion was his relation of election and free will

---

14. E. Gordon Rupp and Philip S. Watson, eds., *Luther and Erasmus: Free Will and Salvation* (Philadelphia: Westminster Press, 1969), 51.

to the character of whole theological systems. For Luther, any form of synergism was a theology of glory, a reason for human pride, rather than a biblical theology of the cross, which crushes all pride. Luther's insistence on the theology of the cross allowed him to argue backward, so to speak, to predestination. The cross of Christ is God's greatest demonstration that man is utterly helpless to attain grace. Insofar as election reinforces man's utter helplessness and God's utter graciousness, it is to that extent a truly Christian doctrine.

There is a reason, though, that a full-fledged Augustinian doctrine of election is now associated much more with Calvin than with Luther. After Luther's death, Philipp Melanchthon, Luther's disciple and heir to the Lutheran Reformation, abandoned his teacher's view of predestination for a gracious synergism anticipatory of Arminianism. In his important *Loci Communes* [*Theological Commonplaces*], Melanchthon teaches that there are three causes of salvation: Scripture, the Holy Spirit, and free will. When asked why one person believes and another does not, Melanchthon answers that "the reason is in us."[15]

John Calvin (1509-64)

Not so John Calvin, the French counterpart to the German Luther. Calvin, the Reformer of Geneva, based his theology on the exposition of Scripture and gave Christ the central place, but with good reason is well known for his highly developed doctrine of election. The systematic statement of Calvin's views is his *Institutes of the Christian Religion*, wherein is found his classic statement on predestination: "In conformity, therefore, to the clear doctrine of Scripture, we assert that by an eternal and immutable counsel God has once for all determined both whom he would admit to salvation and whom he would condemn to destruction."[16]

15. Philipp Melanchthon, 1555 *Loci Communes* (variata).
16. John Calvin, *Institutes of the Christian Religion* 3.21.7, ed. John T. McNeill (Philadelphia: Westminster Press, 1960), 931.

Like the views of the other Reformers, many of Calvin's views were worked out amid heated disputation. On election and free will, his two most important occasional works are *Concerning Free Will* (1543) and *Concerning the Eternal Predestination of God* (1552). Also noteworthy is Calvin's strong sense of continuity with Augustine, of whom he writes, "If I wanted to weave a whole volume from Augustine, I could readily show my readers that I need no other language than his."[17]

When Calvin died, he left his Geneva Academy in the competent hands of Theodore Beza (1519–1605), who was his successor both institutionally and theologically. But although the content of Beza's theology was very much like Calvin's, his method was rather different. Beza was a leading figure in the so-called Protestant scholasticism of the generation after the Reformation, a movement that gave more emphasis to philosophical theology than had Luther and Calvin. Whereas Calvin did not fill in all areas of his theological system, Beza's system was more complete and produced a stronger brand of Calvinism. This strong Calvinism was the one encountered by the students of the Geneva Academy at the end of the sixteenth century, one of whom was a young Dutch ministerial candidate named Jacob Arminius.

Jacob Arminius (1560–1609)

Arminius studied theology at Geneva, under Beza. Upon graduating he returned to his native Amsterdam to take up a call to ministry in the Dutch church. Later, he joined the theological faculty at the University of Leiden. Arminius enjoyed success as a professor, but also drew criticism from his strong Calvinist colleague Franciscus Gomarus. They sparred for some time, until finally Gomarus formally accused Arminius of deviance from the confessional standards of the Dutch church (the Belgic Confession and the Heidelberg Catechism). This crisis caused Arminius to make a systematic statement and defense of his views, in the *Declaration of Sentiments* (1608).

17. Ibid., 942.

Arminius accepted the basic theological approach of his former teacher Beza, but proposed a different understanding of God's plan of salvation. Most importantly, he held that God planned to save those particular people whom he foresees will exercise faith. That is, election to salvation is based on foreseen faith.

Arminius agreed with Calvin's Augustinian view of spiritual inability. But to this he added a doctrine of universal prevenient (preceding) grace. "The grace sufficient for salvation is conferred on the elect and on the non-elect, that, if they will, they may believe or not believe."[18] Whereas for Calvin and Augustine before him prevenient grace was particular and effective, for Arminius it was universal and potential. Like Calvin and Beza, Arminius affirmed divine foreknowledge. But unlike them, he denied that it was a causal force: "A thing does not come to pass because it has been foreknown . . . but it is foreknown . . . because it is yet to come to pass."[19] Rather, the deciding factor in the salvation of a person is that person's free will. The human will is naturally corrupt and unable to choose the good, but universal prevenient grace gives all sinners the ability to exercise saving faith in Christ, if only they will. God foresees what we will freely choose, and elects (or rejects) us according to this foreknowledge.

The Synod of Dort (1618-19)

A few years after Arminius's death, an influential Arminian minority arose among the Dutch Reformed clergy. The Arminian pastors drafted a systematic defense of their views, called the Remonstrance, and the men themselves came to be called the Remonstrants. The Remonstrance was made up of five articles corresponding to the five points of doctrine at the center of the debate:

1. Conditional election
2. Universal atonement

18. Jacob Arminius, *Apology against Thirty-one Theological Articles 28* in *The Works of James Arminius*, trans. James Nichols and William Nichols. 3 vols. (Grand Rapids: Baker, 1999), 2:53.

19. Jacob Arminius, *Private Disputations* 28.14 in ibid., 2:368.

3. Total depravity/prevenient grace
4. Resistible grace
5. Conditional perseverance

Though it is not commonly known, these "five points of Arminianism" preceded the five points of Calvinism. With the five articles of the Remonstrance, the Arminians had made their case, to which the Calvinist majority responded by calling a church synod at Dort in 1618. The Synod of Dort was a general assembly of the Dutch church. Being a court of the church, the synod was not a discussion forum but a deliberative and judicial body, whose purpose was to evaluate and pass judgment on the Remonstrants' views. After deliberation, the synod published its own five points, the five canons of the Synod of Dort, a point-by-point response to the five articles of the Remonstrance. The five canons, in short form, were as follows:

1. Total depravity
2. Unconditional election
3. Limited (i.e., particular) atonement
4. Irresistible grace
5. Perseverance of the saints

Many readers will recognize these five canons as the five points of Calvinism, which in fact originated not with the sixteenth-century French Calvin but with the seventeenth-century Dutch Synod of Dort. The five canons are a Calvinist rebuttal to the Arminianism of the Remonstrance. By publishing them, the Dutch church officially reaffirmed its acceptance of Augustine's view of predestination and judged Arminius's interpretation of the Reformed confessions as out of bounds. In time, the Canons of Dort were added to the Belgic Confession and Heidelberg Catechism to make up the "Three Forms of Unity" of the Reformed Church in the Netherlands and other Reformed churches around the world.

The Modern Period (AD 1700–Present)

The Enlightenment

The birthday of modernism was the European Enlightenment, which came after the Reformation and challenged many of
the basic religious commitments held by Catholics and Protestants.
Two of its hallmarks affected the development of the doctrines of
election and free will. One was the principle of independence from
authority, which expressed itself in the exchange of monarchies
for democracies and of church authority for individual autonomy.
A second hallmark was the priority of reason over revelation, the
privileging of the findings of science over Scripture.

People in the eighteenth century, no less than people today,
experienced a commonsense impression of having libertarian
free will. That is, when we make choices, we typically do not
feel as though the outcomes are determined by external forces.
The upshot in the eighteenth century was the emergence of a
new secular dogma of libertarian free will, also called "absolute
power to the contrary," the complete freedom at any moment to
choose one thing or its opposite, without the involvement of God
or fate in the process. This was not the free will of the ancient
church fathers, but a human freedom built on God's absence
from the universe.

John Wesley (1703–91) and George Whitefield (1714–70)

At Oxford University in England, early in the eighteenth
century, a small group formed for their mutual Christian edification. Two members of the group were brothers, John and Charles
Wesley, and a third was a friend named George Whitefield. Their
classmates teased the members of the "Holy Club," calling them
"methodists" on account of their systematic practice of Christian
disciplines, not realizing that in doing so they were giving a name
to an enduring international church movement.

After taking their degrees at Oxford, the Wesley brothers and
Whitefield sparked the Evangelical Revival in England. But for

28

all their remarkable success in ministry, the friends came to a theological parting of ways. Whitefield held to predestination in the Calvinist tradition, while both the Wesleys were Arminians. Thanks to the strength of their longtime friendship, they parted peacefully, agreeing to go their separate ways.

Whitefield took his preaching ministry across the Atlantic to America, where he became a close friend and influence to Jonathan Edwards of Northampton, Massachusetts, himself a great Calvinist theologian and revival preacher. Together with Edwards, Whitefield sparked the Great Awakening in America, just as he had done with the Wesleys in Britain.

When Whitefield left for America, the Wesleys carried on their ministry in England. Of the two Wesley brothers, John was the preacher and Charles the hymn writer. John is remembered as the founder of Methodism and as one of England's great revival preachers. Less well known is his authorship of a little book titled *Predestination Calmly Considered*, which along with his sermons on free will made John Wesley one of the most articulate and forceful representatives of Arminianism in church history.

What were Wesley's views on the matters before us? He held that there were four proper grounds for belief: Scripture, tradition, reason, and experience (the so-called Wesleyan quadrilateral). By elevating reason and experience alongside Scripture, Wesley gave weight to the commonsense argument for libertarian free will. From tradition, he was influenced by the synergism of the ancient church fathers.

Regarding the doctrine of God, Wesley said that God's primary attribute is love, which he understood to include unwillingness to coerce. Like Arminius before him, Wesley affirmed divine foreknowledge but denied that it was a causal force. Free human actions do not happen because God foreknows them; rather, God foreknows them because they will happen. Regarding sin and grace, Wesley held to the gracious synergism of Arminius: God initiates and human free will chooses to respond or not. Regarding predestination, Wesley held that single predestination necessarily entailed double predestination (the predestination of some to heaven and others to hell). He could not abide the latter, so he had to reject the former. Wesley found the idea of double predestination morally reprehensible. His understanding of God and the gospel was such that he could consistently take only an Arminian view of things, which is why we speak today of Wesleyan Arminianism.

One final word on George Whitefield and John Wesley: the two men are remarkable for their capable articulations of Calvinist and Arminian theology, respectively. But no less remarkable was the quality of their friendship despite their significant theological differences. Wesley preached Whitefield's funeral sermon on November 18, 1770, as Whitefield had requested.[20] They managed what many Christians today cannot seem to—to live charitably together, praying for each other in the cause of the gospel. One wishes that there were more Whitefields among Calvinists, and more Wesleys among Arminians.

Charles Finney (1792–1875)

Understandings of sin and grace were often forged in the fire of revival, as we have seen in the cases of George Whitefield, Jonathan Edwards, and John Wesley. This was true, too, of another important figure a century later: Charles Grandison Finney, the great preacher of the Second Great Awakening. Finney was a preacher through and through, and not a theologian as such, but so great was his influence through the pulpit that he plays a formative role in the story of the doctrine of election.

Finney was an heir of the Arminian/Wesleyan synergistic tradition, but he went several steps beyond either of his esteemed forebears. Finney was "more Arminian than Arminius," holding that the burden is entirely on us to initiate if we would have any gracious exchange with God. This view dovetailed with Finney's pragmatism in the revival movement. He promoted the so-called

20. Arnold A. Dallimore, *George Whitefield: The Life and Times of the Great Evangelist of the Eighteenth Century Revival*, 2 vols. (London: Banner of Truth Trust, 1970–80), 2:510–11.

new measures, various practical means of maximizing response to revival preaching. The burden was on the individual to initiate communication with God, but the preacher could help things along. Many American Christians trace their spiritual heritage back to Finney's revivals.

If Finney was more Arminian than Arminius, it is also true that some advocates of predestination have been more Calvinist than Calvin. The next chapter in the story involves a case of "hyper-Calvinism."

Charles Haddon Spurgeon (1834–92) and the "Hyperists"

Charles Haddon Spurgeon was raised in a rural Congregationalist church that was basically Calvinist in theology. At twenty he was ordained to the ministry in the Particular Baptist denomination and called to the pulpit of New Park Street Church in London. Upon arriving at the church, Spurgeon quickly found himself in controversy.

In London, Spurgeon encountered "Hyperism," whose main points can be briefly sketched. First, God loves the elect, but not the nonelect. Second, there is no such thing as a universal gospel call, but only an effective call to the elect. Third, strictly speaking, unbelief is not a sin because the nonelect cannot possibly exercise saving faith. Fourth, anything short of this degree of Calvinism is sub-Christian.

Here was a system of extreme Calvinism, in which divine agency completely overwhelms any hint of human agency. For this reason Spurgeon called it "Hyperism" and others since have called it "hyper-Calvinism." Leading Hyperist James Wells published scathing criticisms of Spurgeon in Particular Baptist magazines. To the disappointment of many, Spurgeon responded only in his sermons. First of all, he said, his particular electing love notwithstanding, God has a general love for all mankind. Second, the gospel call is indeed universal. "[The Hyperists] are too orthodox to obey the Master's will; they desire to understand first who are appointed to come to the supper, and then they will invite them."[21] Third and finally, Christ invites any who will to come to him; therefore, those who reject him bring down judgment on themselves. Thus Spurgeon restated for his people the old view of predestination held by Augustine and Calvin.

In the end, due in part to Spurgeon's excellence as a preacher, traditional Calvinism came to enjoy wider approval among the Particular Baptists in England. The Hyperists became little more than an entrenched minority. In the broader theater of English evangelicalism, however, by the end of the nineteenth century, Calvinism had waned and Arminianism prevailed. But it mattered little because by this time neither party was concerned about the other; instead, both were concerned about a third party that was rapidly becoming more influential than either of them.

We have talked briefly about the European Enlightenment and the new secular dogma of libertarian free will. It took some time, but when the seeds of the Enlightenment took root in the soil of the church, the flower that bloomed was called liberal Protestantism (or simply liberalism). With the rise of liberalism, the story of election and free will takes a curious turn because liberalism represented a general departure from all the traditional topics of systematic theology.

Friedrich Schleiermacher (1768–1834)

For the doctrine of election, there is no better example of this tendency than the work of the German theologian Friedrich Schleiermacher, who wrote at the turn of the nineteenth century and is known as the father of classic liberal theology. He said about the extent of God's election, "If . . . we proceed on the definite assumption that all belonging to the human race are eventually taken up into living fellowship with Christ, there is nothing for it but this single divine foreordination."[22]

---

21. Charles Haddon Spurgeon, *Metropolitan Tabernacle Pulpit*, 63 vols. (Pasadena, TX: Pilgrim Publications, 1969–80), 11:495.
22. Friedrich Schleiermacher, *The Christian Faith*, ed. H. R. Mackintosh and J. S. Stewart (Edinburgh: T&T Clark, 1928), 549.

Note that he states as a "definite assumption" the idea that all persons will be saved. But we know from our survey of the doctrine that this is to beg the question at the heart of the ancient "problem of predestination." The difficulty is precisely how God could choose some and reject others. But Schleiermacher cut this Gordian knot with a single throwaway phrase, assuming from the outset that God could not possibly reject anyone. Not surprisingly, many in the church were troubled about the changes introduced by liberalism, but it was not until the early part of the twentieth century, again in Europe, that a figure arose to challenge those changes on a grand scale.

Karl Barth (1886–1968)

Karl Barth was a minister in the Reformed Church of Switzerland and as such stood in the Reformed and predestinarian tradition of John Calvin. Contrary to some conservative misrepresentations, Barth was not a theological liberal. On the contrary, his life's work was motivated by a sharp departure from the liberalism of the previous generation. Having been trained by a liberal theological faculty, the young pastor Barth became dissatisfied with the theology his professors had taught him, finding it inadequate to deal with not only the biblical story but also life as his parishioners experienced it.

But Barth's departure from liberalism was not simply a return to one of the older traditions. He was not a liberal, nor was he an Arminian, but neither was he a traditional Calvinist. He complained that his own theological tradition—the view of predestination held by Augustine, Thomas, and Calvin—abstracted the principle of election from Christ. Barth put forth a more christocentric doctrine of predestination.

He went so far as to affirm double predestination (predestination of some to heaven and others to hell), but with a christocentric twist. For Barth, it is *Christ* who is doubly predestined, in that he is both the elect Man and the reprobate Man. Election and reprobation (God's predestination of sinners to condemnation),

33

Barth said, properly pertain not to us but to Christ. He wrote, "In the election of Jesus Christ which is the eternal will of God, God has ascribed to man . . . election, salvation and life; and to himself he has ascribed . . . reprobation, perdition and death."[23] Predestination thus applies not to distinct sets of people but to the whole human race in Christ. Barth saw in this a solution to the age-old problem of election that avoided the errors of Calvin on the one hand and Schleiermacher on the other.

To his credit, Barth challenged the dominance of theological liberalism in the first half of the twentieth century. But concerning predestination, the question arises whether Barth really avoided the universalism of Schleiermacher. If election applies to the whole human race in Christ and reprobation applies to Christ as the sin-bearer, then it looks as though everyone is saved in the end. Although Barth expressly denied that he was a universalist, the logic of his position points in that direction.

Today

In current evangelicalism, the heirs of Calvin and Arminius continue to debate. In American pews, Arminianism may still predominate, but in seminaries and publishing houses, Calvinism is gaining ground. For example, of recent systematic theologies, the top two best sellers take a Calvinist view of sin and grace.[24]

Another development was the 2004 publication by InterVarsity Press of the companion volumes *Why I Am Not a Calvinist* (by Jerry L. Walls and Joseph R. Dongell of Asbury Seminary) and *Why I Am Not an Arminian* (by Robert A. Peterson and Michael D. Williams of Covenant Seminary). These volumes represent a renewed effort at respectful dialogue between Calvinists and Arminians, a dialogue welcomed by many evangelicals.

23. Karl Barth, *Church Dogmatics*, ed. G. W. Bromiley and T. F. Torrance, vol. 2, pt. 2 (London: T & T International, 2004), 163.
24. On August 23, 2006, according to Amazon.com, they were: Wayne Grudem, *Systematic Theology* (Grand Rapids: Zondervan, 1994) and Millard J. Erickson, *Christian Theology*, 2nd ed. (Grand Rapids: Baker, 1998).

What does the future hold for election and free will? Among evangelicals, it is reasonable to expect ongoing debate along basically Calvinist and Arminian lines. We can hope, however, that we might reclaim the legacy of peaceable disagreement left by Wesley and Whitefield. Meanwhile, in the mainline churches there is a new openness to old doctrines, in the form of various confessing church movements and of postliberal theology in mainline seminaries and divinity schools. This suggests that the church might again enjoy broader discussion (in terms both of parties present and of positions expressed) on these important doctrines.

Conclusion

We have told the story of election and free will from the second-century apostolic fathers down to our day. Where does this leave us? Perhaps most importantly, we have seen that both "Calvinism" and "Arminianism," in spite of their Reformation-era names, are in fact quite ancient. The issue of monergism versus synergism goes all the way back to the early church; there simply is no historic Christian consensus on this matter. We are not dealing with a doctrine such as the Trinity or the two natures of Christ, which the ecumenical councils settled once and for all in the early centuries. Rather, within the fold of orthodoxy there is a whole range of positions on election and free will. At the least, this means that it is wrong for Calvinists and Arminians to condemn one another.

We have also seen that a critical factor in the story is people's reasons for holding the views they do. When it comes to why we hold certain beliefs, we are influenced by contemporary context and personal psychology as well as biblical conviction. Often our views on any issue are influenced by other things that are especially important to us. So, for example, Pelagius took an idiosyncratic view of human freedom because he had such a zealous concern for Christian obedience. Martin Luther, captured by the utter graciousness of God in justification, held to a view

35

of predestination that reinforced that principle. Charles Finney's concern for promoting the nineteenth-century revivals helped shape his views of human initiative and divine aid.

This does not mean that any of these views are wrong because people have complex reasons for holding them, nor that we should despair of knowing what the Bible teaches because other factors have muddied the waters. Rather, the history of the doctrine shows the need for every generation to go back again to Scripture, to hear God's Word on its own terms. That is the principal undertaking of this book, and to it we now turn.

Election in the
Old Testament

The story of Israel is based on the belief that from out of all
the nations of the world God has, in his grace, chosen Israel
to be his own people . . . In theological terms this is belief
in the "election" of a particular group of people . . . Election
is imbedded in the biblical narrative from the account of the
call of Abraham onward . . . While it is primarily Israel that is
chosen, God also calls individuals to serve him in and through
his people.[1]

The goal of our study of election is to explore the New
Testament's teaching that God chose individuals and the church.
But in our attempt to understand the Bible's teaching, we do
not begin with the New Testament. Instead, we start at the
beginning of the biblical story. The Old Testament has much to
teach us concerning election and will help us begin to answer
the following important questions: Whom does God choose?
On what basis does he choose them? For what purposes does
he choose them? The Old Testament speaks of God's choice of
individuals, focuses on his election of the nation of Israel, and
mentions once his choosing the Messiah. Therefore, we will
consider God's election of:

1. Charles H. H. Scobie, *The Ways of Our God: An Approach to Biblical Theology* (Grand Rapids: Eerdmans, 2003), 470.

- Individuals
- The Nation of Israel
- The Messiah

The Election of Individuals

Abraham

A striking example of election in the Old Testament is God's choosing of Abraham. Nehemiah 9:7 recalls that God did this: "You are the LORD, the God who chose Abram and brought him out of Ur of the Chaldeans and gave him the name Abraham." In his last address to the Israelites before his death, Joshua provides important background for understanding Abraham's election. "Thus says the LORD, the God of Israel, 'Long ago, your fathers lived beyond the Euphrates, Terah, the father of Abraham and of Nahor; and they served other gods. Then I took your father Abraham from beyond the River and led him through all the land of Canaan, and made his offspring many'" (Josh. 24:2–3).

Abraham, "the man of faith" (Gal. 3:9) and revered father of the Jewish nation, comes from a family of idolaters! And had the Lord not intervened, he would have continued the family tradition and been an idolater himself. But God calls Abram from Ur, commands him to leave his country, people, and father's household, and promises to bless him, and through him the world (Gen. 12:1–3). Later, God promises to protect Abram (to be his "shield") and promises that the result of his life of faith would be a very great reward (Gen. 15:1). When God promises to give Abram countless offspring, "he believed the LORD, and he counted it to him as righteousness" (Gen. 15:6). God enters into a covenant with Abram, and in a solemn ceremony God swears that he would curse himself before he would break his promises to Abram (Gen. 15:12–19)!

In Genesis 17, God changes this man's name from "Abram" ("exalted father") to "Abraham" ("father of many") and swears, "I will establish my covenant between me and you and your offspring after you throughout their generations for an everlasting covenant, to be God to you and to your offspring after you" (Gen. 17:7). Although the covenant pertains to the land of Canaan and circumcision, our present focus is on God's committing himself to Abraham and his descendants forever.

God, the Creator of all things, makes Abram (Josh. 24:3), a son of idolaters, the father of the covenant nation. This means that God's choice of him is all of grace, for on his own Abram never would have chosen God. In fact, God chooses someone ignorant of the true God to highlight his grace and saving initiative. God claims Abram for himself and promises to grant him great blessings. In sovereign electing graces he pledges to be God to Abraham and his offspring. Statements such as the following, therefore, are wrongheaded: "What [God] is certainly *not* doing is choosing Abraham to receive personal redemption and leaving the rest to perish."[2] In fact, God chooses Abraham, out of all the idolaters in the world, for salvation and to be the father of the covenant nation that will ultimately through Christ bring salvation to the world. Although the claim has been made that election is for service rather than salvation, the truth is that election is for both. Abraham is called by God to salvation, as we have shown (Gen. 15:1, 6; 17:7). And Abraham is called by God to serve him (among other ways) by moving to Canaan (Gen. 12:1, 4), interceding for Sodom (Gen. 18:22–33), and offering Isaac (Gen. 22:1–14).

Jacob

The Lord answers Isaac's prayer and causes his wife, Rebekah, to become pregnant with twins (Gen. 25:21–22). When she asks the Lord for an explanation as the babies moved violently within her womb, he provides one: "Two nations are in your womb, and two peoples from within you shall be divided; the one shall be stronger than the other, the older shall serve the younger" (Gen. 25:23). Rebekah's two babies are named Esau

2. Roger T. Forster and V. Paul Marston, *God's Strategy in Human History* (Wheaton: Tyndale House, 1973), 51.

and Jacob. According to J. Barton Payne, Jacob is "the most out-standing example of unconditional election to be found in all of Scripture."[3] Payne explains why he reaches this conclusion:

> He was chosen before birth. He was one of twins, so humanly equal. He was the younger of the two and, in his personal character, he was an unethical trickster—from his very birth in fact . . . God even granted him the promise of the testament at the very moment he was fleeing from home as a result of his crimes (Gen. 28:15).[4]

It is right to point out that Jacob and Esau represent nations, even while within their mother's womb, as the quotation of Genesis 25:23 above confirms (cf. Mal. 1:2–3). But it is wrong to conclude from that fact that God fails to deal with the twins as individuals, too, as some have claimed.[5] We know this because Paul explained:

> When Rebecca had conceived children by one man, our forefa-ther Isaac, though they were not yet born and had done nothing either good or bad—*in order that God's purpose of election might continue*, not because of works but because of his call—she was told, "The older will serve the younger." As it is written, "Jacob I loved, but Esau I hated." (Rom. 9:10–13)

To summarize: God deals with Jacob and Esau both as indi-viduals and as the fathers of nations. He chooses Jacob as an individual to be a special recipient of his love *and* chooses him to be heir of his promises to the nation. Therefore, Malachi employs the words "I have loved Jacob but Esau I have hated" to refer to the nations of Israel and Edom, respectively (Mal. 1:2–3), while Paul employs the same words in Romans 9:13 to refer to Jacob as chosen by God and Esau as rejected, as the preceding words

3. J. Barton Payne, *The Theology of the Older Testament* (Grand Rapids: Zondervan, 1962), 179.
4. Ibid.
5. Forster and Marston, *God's Strategy*, 60–61.

in Romans 9 demonstrate. The apostle is unambiguous: God chooses Jacob and rejects Esau before birth "in order that God's purpose of election might continue, not because of works but because of his call" (Rom. 9:11).

The Election of the Nation of Israel

> Blessed is the nation whose God is the LORD,
>> the people whom he has chosen as his heritage! (Ps. 33:12)

> But you, Israel, my servant,
>> Jacob, whom I have chosen,
>> the offspring of Abraham, my friend;
> you whom I took from the ends of the earth,
>> and called from its farthest corners,
> saying to you, "You are my servant,
>> I have chosen you and not cast you off";
> fear not, for I am with you;
>> be not dismayed, for I am your God;
> I will strengthen you, I will help you,
>> I will uphold you with my righteous right hand. (Isa. 41:8–10)

The Old Testament refers to God's election of individuals, but it centers on his choice of Israel. While mentioning other texts, we will concentrate on four passages in Deuteronomy: 4:37–38; 7:6–8; 10:14–15; and 14:2.

Deuteronomy 4:37–38

Moses charges the Israelites to acknowledge the Lord alone as God

> because he loved your fathers and chose their offspring after them and brought you out of Egypt with his own presence, by his great power, driving out before you nations greater and mightier than yourselves, to bring you in, to give you their land for an inheritance, as it is this day.

41

God loves and chooses Israel. The bond between God's love and election forges a biblical pattern, a pattern found in both Testaments. For example, Paul writes, "In love he [God the Father] predestined us for adoption through Jesus Christ" (Eph. 1:4–5). Moreover, God delivers the Israelites from Egyptian slavery because of his love for and choice of Israel. Scripture links God's election of the nation with his redeeming of it. This reflects another biblical pattern—presenting election as the cause of redemption.

Deuteronomy 7:6–8

God declares the following as he commands the Israelites to drive the pagan nations out of Canaan:

> For you are a people holy to the LORD your God. The LORD your God has chosen you to be a people for his treasured possession, out of all the peoples who are on the face of the earth. It was not because you were more in number than any other people that the LORD set his love on you and chose you, for you were the fewest of all peoples, but it is because the LORD loves you and is keeping the oath that he swore to your fathers, that the LORD has brought you out with a mighty hand and redeemed you from the house of slavery, from the hand of Pharaoh king of Egypt.

This passage is saturated with teaching about election. It explains why God chooses Israel, negatively and positively. He does not choose the nation because of its great numbers, for Israel was small (v. 7). This is an Old Testament way of saying that God's choice of Israel is not based on merit. God could have chosen a large, accomplished, or prestigious nation, but instead he chooses a nation to which none of these adjectives apply. He does so to magnify his own name. The New Testament expresses the same idea: "But God chose what is foolish in the world to shame the wise; God chose what is weak in the world to shame the strong; God chose what is low and despised in the world, even things that are not, to bring to nothing things that are, so that no human being might boast in the presence of God" (1 Cor. 1:27–29).

The positive reason for God's choice is also given—because he loves Israel. His choice is a choice of love. As in Deuteronomy 4:37, so here Israel's election is based on God's affection and love (Deut. 7:7–8). This is an important biblical principle: God chooses people because he loves them (cf. 2 Tim. 1:9).

Moreover, God's choice of Israel is exclusive. Verse 6 repeats, "The LORD your God has chosen you to be a people for his treasured possession, out of all the peoples who are on the face of the earth." God could have chosen another nation instead of Israel, or he could have chosen more than one nation. Instead, he chooses it and it alone—out of all the nations—to be his covenant people. No further explanation is given except that God chooses according to his love and will. Election is therefore mysterious.

God grants some privileges only to his elect nation. Included among these is the fact that Israel is God's people (Deut. 7:6): of all nations, it alone belongs to him. In addition, it is his peculiar treasure. "The word means 'special treasure' belonging privately to a king (e.g. 1 Chron. 29:3). This implies special value as well as special relationship."[6] The great King's choice of Israel invests the nation with special value and special relationship to him.

God's electing love for Israel also brings the special responsibility of holiness. God sets Israel apart as a holy nation responsible to live up to its calling (Deut. 7:6). It must reject the false religions of the Canaanites (vv. 1–5) and do God's will (v. 11). This, too, is a scriptural pattern—election brings with it great responsibility to those whom God chooses.

Deuteronomy 10:14–15

Moses instructs the Israelites to fear, obey, love, and serve the Lord with their whole hearts. Then he says:

6. R. Alan Cole, *Exodus*, Tyndale Old Testament Commentaries (London: Tyndale, 1973), 144.

> Behold, to the LORD your God belong heaven and the heaven
> of heavens, the earth with all that is in it. Yet the LORD set his
> heart in love on your fathers and chose their offspring after
> them, you above all peoples, as you are this day.

It is remarkable that even though God owns everything that exists, he still loves and chooses Israel (Deut. 10:15). Consequently, Israel's election is a great privilege. Here again God's love and election are joined (v. 15). Once more God's exclusive choice of Israel "above all peoples" is taught (v. 15). And once more we see that God's choice brings responsibility; Israel's election is intended to produce results. The elect people are to "circumcise" their "heart" and humble themselves before God (v. 16). They are to love aliens in their midst, to fear God and serve him alone (vv. 19–20).

Deuteronomy 14:2

> The LORD has chosen you to be a people for his treasured
> possession, out of all the peoples who are on the face of the
> earth.

Because this text repeats earlier themes, we will treat it briefly. God chooses Israel alone out of all the nations and makes it his peculiar treasure. Because the surrounding verses urge Israel to live in a holy manner, once again God combines election and holiness. We will summarize Deuteronomy's teaching concerning God's choice of Israel after treating one more topic.

The Election of the Messiah

A minor theme in the Old Testament, but one that has great significance in the Bible's story overall, is Isaiah's teaching that the Messiah is chosen by God. When Isaiah writes of the servant of the Lord, he sometimes refers to the nation of Israel and sometimes to its promised Messiah. In Isaiah 42:1 the prophet says: "Behold my servant, whom I uphold, *my chosen*, in whom my soul delights; I have put my Spirit upon him; he will bring forth justice to the nations." The New Testament understands these words as speaking of the Messiah.

After Jesus heals a man with a withered hand on the Sabbath, the Pharisees conspire to destroy Jesus. In response he withdraws, to avoid further conflict. Still, many people follow him, and he heals them, but instructs them not to spread abroad the news of their healing. Matthew writes, "This was to fulfill what was spoken by the prophet Isaiah," and then quotes Isaiah 42:1–3, beginning with verse 1, "Behold, my servant whom I have *chosen*" (Matt. 12:17–18). Matthew views Jesus' desire not to publicize his ministry as fulfilling Isaiah's words, "He will not quarrel or cry aloud, nor will anyone hear his voice in the streets; a bruised reed he will not break, and a smoldering wick he will not quench" (Matt. 12:19–20, quoting Isa. 42:2–3). In the process Matthew identifies Jesus with the chosen servant of Isaiah 42:1.

Isaiah speaks of an elect individual whom God would send to bring justice to the nations; Matthew identifies Jesus as that prophesied elect servant of God. The Messiah's election is both similar and dissimilar to that of other individuals in the Old Testament. Like them, he is chosen by God to serve God. Unlike them, he does not need a Savior but is the Savior. As we will see, the New Testament teaches more about Christ's being chosen; for now, we note that the roots of this teaching sink deep into the soil of Isaiah's prophecy.

Conclusion

Conclusions follow from our investigation of God's election in the Old Testament. We learn of both individual and corporate election: God chooses Abraham and Jacob, and he also chooses the nation of Israel. It is a mistake, therefore, to regard individual and corporate election as incompatible.

Election is both individual and corporate. God chooses Abram and Jacob and from them brings forth a chosen nation. Geerhardus Vos says it well: "The election of Abraham . . . was meant as a particularistic means towards a universalistic end."[7] We will see that the New Testament also teaches individual and corporate election.

The Individual Election of Abraham and Jacob

Our investigation of God's choice of Abraham and Jacob yields theological dividends.

Individual Election Is for Salvation and Service. First, although Arminians sometimes teach that God elects individuals for service but not for salvation, God does both. He chooses Abram for salvation because God promises to be Abraham's God (Gen. 17:7). God also chooses Abram for service when he orders him to leave his home and go to Canaan (Gen. 12:1) and when he tells him to offer Isaac as a sacrifice (Gen. 22:2).

The Jacob narrative demonstrates the same pattern. God chooses him before birth (Gen. 25:23; Rom. 9:11–12) to serve God as the heir of the promises made to Abraham and Isaac. As a result, in the Old Testament God's words "Jacob I loved" speak of the nation Israel that God would bring from Jacob (Mal. 1:2; God changed Jacob's name to "Israel" in Gen. 32:28). In the New Testament the same words speak of God's electing and saving love for Jacob as an individual (Rom. 9:10–13).

Individual Election Is Based on God's Love and Will. A second theological truth follows: God's love and will are the basis of Abraham's and Jacob's election. God does not elect them on the basis of foreseen merit or foreseen faith. We know this because Abram is an idolater when God chooses him (Josh. 24:2–3). It is important to note that God's choice of his people

7. Geerhardus Vos, *Biblical Theology* (Grand Rapids: Eerdmans, 1948), 90.

is based on his will *and* his love. "In Genesis 12 the choice of Abraham is totally unexpected and unexplained; it depends entirely on divine initiative, divine grace, and divine love."[8]

If someone were trying to find an example of election based on foreseen faith or holiness, Jacob would make a poor choice. "God's grace selects this terribly imperfect man and not because of merit on his part."[9] Jacob's sins are not hidden by the Old Testament story. His scheming (Gen. 25:31–33), deceit (Gen. 27:19, 24, 35; 31:20), and cowardice (Gen. 26:7; 31:31; 33:3, 8) are well known. Jacob's story disproves the notion that God's choice of individuals is based on faith or holiness. Instead, Jacob's story highlights the fact that God's choice of individuals *produces* faith and holiness. Indeed, it is not until Jacob returns to Bethel (Gen. 35:9–15) that he wholeheartedly commits himself to the God of his fathers, the God who more than twenty years before had graciously committed himself to Jacob.

The Corporate Election of Israel

The prime example of election in the Old Testament is God's choosing the nation of Israel. Here are five key points:

Election Is Both Individual and Corporate. First, it is wrong to pit individual and corporate election against each other, as Jack Cottrell does when he writes, "The election of Israel was the election of a group or a corporate body, not the election of individuals."[10] Rather, the story of Abraham shows that they go together. God chooses Abram as an individual, but "election in this case proves God's merciful kindness to the world, not just to Abram."[11] From Abraham God brings

8. Scobie, *The Ways of Our God*, 471.
9. Paul R. House, *Old Testament Theology* (Downers Grove, IL: InterVarsity Press, 1998), 78.
10. Jack Cottrell, "Conditional Election," in *Grace Unlimited*, ed. Clark H. Pinnock (Minneapolis: Bethany House, 1975), 53.
11. House, *Old Testament Theology*, 73.

the elect nation of Israel, and from Israel he brings the Christ through whom the promise to Abram is fulfilled: "In you shall all the nations be blessed" (Gal. 3:8, quoting Gen. 12:3).

God's Election of Israel Is Based on His Grace. Second is the reason for God's election of Israel. God does not choose Israel because of its large size; it is a small nation (Deut. 7:7). God does not survey the nations and choose the largest, most prosperous one, the one with the most potential. Instead, he chooses one that is tiny and with little potential, humanly speaking. This is another way of saying that Israel's election is based on grace. In fact, three times we read that God loves Israel and chooses it (Deut. 4:37; 7:7–8; 10:15). Writing from an Arminian perspective, William Klein agrees:

> What motivated God to choose Israel? The Old Testament writers overwhelmingly assert that Israel could not attribute her election to anything within the nation herself. Beginning with God's selection of the patriarch Abraham (Gen. 18:18–19; cf. 12:1–4; 17:1–8; Deut. 4:37), Israel owes its existence as God's people solely to his gracious, unmerited choice . . . God's lovingkindness alone can explain his choice.[12]

The idea that God chooses Israel because he sees something (present or future) in it does not square with the Old Testament picture, which repeatedly presents it as a rebellious people, whom God loves in spite of their stubbornness. Israel's election is not based on God's foreseeing its faith, but on God's free grace. Brevard Childs underscores this truth: "That the choice of Israel derives 'solely from the mysterious and inexplicable love of God' is a major theme of the Deuteronomic reflection on the meaning of election."[13]

---

12. William W. Klein, *The New Chosen People: A Corporate View of Election* (Grand Rapids: Academie Books, 1990), 29–30.

13. Brevard Childs, *Biblical Theology of the Old and New Testaments: Theological Reflections on the Christian Bible* (Minneapolis: Fortress Press, 1992), 426, quoted in Scobie, *The Ways of Our God*, 472.

God's Election of Israel Is Particular. Third is the particularity of Israel's election. Moses says three times that God chooses Israel out of all the nations (Deut. 7:6; 10:15; 14:2). God does not choose every nation in Old Testament times. He does not choose Egypt or Assyria or Babylon; rather, he chooses Israel. The Israelites received benefits from God not conferred on other nations. Some would consider this unfair, but the Old Testament does not view it that way. Indeed, in the very context of confessing God's unique choice of Israel, the text says, "The LORD your God is God of gods and Lord of lords, the great, the mighty, and the awesome God, *who is not partial* and takes no bribe" (Deut. 10:17).

A distinction made by John Frame between historical and eternal election is helpful.[14] God's choice of the nation of Israel is an example of *historical election*—although God chooses Israel, his choice does not necessarily result in the salvation of every Israelite. Those who rebel against him and disregard his covenant are lost. Similarly, God chooses via historical election the visible New Testament church as a corporate people, but not every individual in the church is saved. By contrast, *eternal election* is election that always results in salvation, as, for example, God's choice of individuals for salvation as revealed in the New Testament. Both historical election and eternal election are forms of election in that both involve God's choices. But differences between them are clarified by Frame's statement, "All of the eternally elect are historically elect, but not vice versa."[15] Historical election puts one within the community of faith, but does not guarantee that one has been eternally elected for salvation. Elect individuals ultimately believe and obey God.

God's Election of Israel Is Not Arbitrary. Fourth, we must answer the charge of arbitrariness. At times Arminian writers have labeled the Calvinist understanding of predestination

14. John Frame, *The Doctrine of God* (Phillipsburg, NJ: P&R Publishing, 2002), 317–30.
15. Ibid., 329.

as arbitrary. As we saw in Deuteronomy, the reason for God's choosing Israel to be his covenant people out of all the nations on the face of the earth lies in God's love and will. Does that make God's election of Israel arbitrary? Not at all. If we search for reasons behind God's love and will as to why God chose Israel, we will find that Scripture is silent. God does not answer every question that we might ask. We must trust God's character in revealing to us what he wants us to know and leave "the secret things . . . to the LORD our God" (Deut. 29:29). God's election of Israel is not arbitrary; it is based on his love and will. Beyond that it is unwise for us to inquire.

God's Election of Israel Produces Results. Fifth, the results of Israel's election include ownership, redemption, and responsibility. God chose Israel to be his own people, his peculiar treasure (Deut. 7:6; 14:2). Among all the nations on earth, Israel alone belongs to the Lord by covenant. Furthermore, God redeemed the Israelites from Egyptian bondage because he loved and chose them (Deut. 4:37; 7:6). Election resulted in redemption. In addition, because the Lord chose Israel, it is to live as a holy nation (Deut. 7:1–6; 14:1–2), to fear and serve the Lord and love aliens (Deut. 10:19–20). That is, precisely because the Lord chooses Israel to be his nation, it has greater responsibility than do the other nations. Charles Scobie underlines this point:

> Being God's chosen people does not mean that he will judge them less severely. On the contrary, since God's will has been more clearly revealed to them and they have been chosen to serve God in a special way, their failures will bring greater condemnation. . . . Election and covenant are the basic presuppositions of the prophets' messages of judgment. Nowhere is this more forcefully put than in Amos 3:2, where God says to Israel: "You only have I known of all the families of the earth; *therefore* I will punish you for all your iniquities."[16]

16. Scobie, *The Ways of Our God*, 472–73 (italics in original).

The Election of the Messiah

Finally, we saw that the Old Testament in Isaiah 42:1 predicts that the coming servant of the Lord, the Messiah, will be chosen by God for his mission. This reference teases us, making us want to learn more. And learn more we shall when we turn to the New Testament, where the predicted Messiah appears on the scene.

In the meantime, locating Christ in the biblical story of election forms a fitting end to this chapter and segue to the next one. The story begins when the Old Testament speaks of God's election of individuals, but its major concern is his choice of the nation of Israel. Overall the nation fails in its responsibilities to glorify God and be a light to the other nations. God therefore sends it into captivity, first the northern kingdom of Israel in 722 BC, and then the southern kingdom of Judah in 586 BC. But God does not give up on the nation or go back on his promises to the patriarchs. Instead, he sends one Israelite who would succeed where the chosen nation had failed—the Lord Jesus Christ. In fact, as we have seen, the Old Testament had predicted that the Messiah would be chosen of God. This Messiah lives a sinless life, culminating in his death and resurrection, which secures salvation for every believer. He also teaches concerning many themes, including election—not only of Jews but also of Gentiles. After he returns to heaven, he and the Father send the Spirit, who, among other ministries, fulfills Jesus' promises by leading the apostles whom he had chosen to write the New Testament (John 14:26; 16:13). The New Testament completes the Bible's doctrine of predestination by teaching in the gospels, Acts, the epistles, and Revelation that God chooses many individuals, both Jews and Gentiles, to constitute the Christian church. It is Christ himself who forges the theological link between the Old Testament election of the nation of Israel and the New Testament election of the church.

Election in the
Gospels and Acts

After surveying election in the Old Testament, we now turn our attention to the New Testament. We begin with:

- The Synoptic Gospels (Matthew, Mark, and Luke)
- The Gospel of John
- The Acts of the Apostles

A primary truth concerning election conveyed in these books is that God has chosen a people for himself. We also learn that God chose Jesus as the incarnate Redeemer. In addition, in one passage in the gospel of John, Jesus is portrayed as the author of election.

Election in the Synoptic Gospels

The first three gospels advance the biblical story by introducing election in the New Testament. They do not often speak of election, but when they do, they tell of God's choice of a people and of his choice of Jesus to be the servant of the Lord prophesied by Isaiah.

The Election of the People of God

Mark 13:20–27. Jesus' famous prophetic discourse in Mark 13 (and its parallel in Matthew 24:22, 24, 31) contains three references to persons chosen for salvation. In a manner reminiscent of Old Testament prophets, Jesus predicts events near and far in the same message: the destruction of Jerusalem in AD 70 and his own second coming at the end of the age. He warns of trouble such as the world has not seen from its creation by God until now. In fact, things will get so bad that "if the Lord had not cut short the days, no human being would be saved. But for the sake of *the elect, whom he chose*, he shortened the days" (Mark 13:20). The purpose for which God will reduce the length of the terrible times ahead is to protect his chosen people. Jesus teaches that God has chosen some people and will act on their behalf to lessen the intensity of the coming tribulation.

He warns his hearers not to be easily misled when they hear of sightings of pseudo-messiahs: "False christs and false prophets will arise and perform signs and wonders, to lead astray, if possible, *the elect*" (Mark 13:22). Once more Jesus teaches that God has chosen people and will protect them. Here he promises to keep them from being duped by the miracles of the false christs who are sure to appear.

I. Howard Marshall explores two possibilities. First, if the words "if possible" in Mark 13:22 express the mind of the deceivers, then the possibility of apostasy is left open. But second, if the words "if possible" express Jesus' mind, then "it is denied that the possibility exists." Marshall concludes, "The possibility that the elect may be led astray cannot be ruled out, although the form of expression certainly suggests that the possibility is a remote one."[1] But Marshall is in error on this point; the possibility is not even remote. The words "if possible" are more naturally interpreted as expressing Jesus' mind. I say this because Jesus is the speaker for Mark 13:14–20 and he carefully introduces words of deceivers in v. 21: "And then if anyone says to you, 'Look, here is the Christ!' or 'Look, there he is!' do not believe it." He then continues to warn his hearers about deceivers in verses 22–23. Therefore, Leon Morris rightly summarizes Jesus' teaching: "Since

1. Howard Marshall, *Kept by the Power of God: A Study of Perseverance and Falling Away* (London: Epworth Press, 1969), 54.

the elect are God's own, and are kept by the power of God, it will not be possible for them to be led away by these charlatans."[2]

Jesus does not intend for his hearers to take their ease as a result of his sharing that God will protect them. Rather, he urges them to be spiritually prepared in light of the second coming. At that time, he promises, he will return "with great power and glory. And then he will send out the angels and gather *his elect* from the four winds, from the ends of the earth to the ends of heaven" (Mark 13:26–27). These are the people whom God has chosen—"his elect." Clearly, they are chosen for salvation because the returning Son of Man will gather them to share in his kingdom.

The election that Jesus speaks about in Mark 13 differs in two ways from the election of Israel in the Old Testament. First, it does not include all Jews. We say that because (keeping in mind that Jesus was speaking to a Jewish audience) families are split over Christ (Mark 13:12) and some Jews will persecute believers (13:9). Here, as in chapter 3 on election in the Old Testament, we distinguish between "historical election" and "eternal election." Israel as a nation was elected historically and included both saved and lost persons. The election of which Jesus speaks here is an eternal election because all persons so chosen are saved. Writing from an Arminian perspective, William Klein agrees: "The 'elect' here are genuine disciples—God's people, those he has chosen and whom he will save at the Parousia (Matt. 24:27, 37, 39)."[3] The second way in which the election of which Jesus speaks is different from the election of Israel is that it includes Gentiles: the gospel must first be preached to all the nations (Mark 13:10), and the elect are gathered "from the four winds, from the ends of the earth to the ends of heaven" (13:27).

Matthew 22:14. The emphasis of the parable of the wedding banquet is not on divine sovereignty in salvation. Instead, the

---

2. Leon Morris, *The Gospel according to Matthew* (Grand Rapids: Eerdmans, 1992), 607.
3. William W. Klein, *The New Chosen People: A Corporate View of Election* (Grand Rapids: Academie Books, 1990), 66–67.

parable teaches God's gracious invitation to all to enter his kingdom (represented by the banquet) and the folly of rejecting that
invitation. Those who come to the banquet unprepared share the
same terrible fate as those who spurn God's offer: they are cast
"into the outer darkness" where "there will be weeping and gnash-
ing of teeth" (Matt. 22:13). So Jesus' parable emphasizes grace,
human responsibility, and hell. But lest readers think things have
gotten out of God's control, Jesus ends the parable on a note of divine sovereignty: "For many are called, but few are chosen" (Matt.
22:14). Viewed in the light of the Old Testament, this means: "The
center of gravity in the notion of election had shifted from God's
choice of the whole nation of Israel (so the Old Testament) to that
of the righteous remnant in the nation."[4] It is unwise to draw too
much from this tantalizing saying, but we note that it distinguishes the "chosen" from others. Not everyone (even in the chosen
nation of Israel) is chosen in the way of which Jesus speaks here—
chosen to belong to the kingdom of God in its final form.

William Klein holds that here Jesus explains why God
chooses some and not others:

> The chosen ones are marked out because they alone responded
> to the invitation *in the proper way*. . . . People acquire "chosen-
> ness" at some point in their lives. The Jews had every opportunity
> to enter the sphere of the elect, but they refused God's invita-
> tions. The disciples accepted the invitation and are therefore
> among the chosen few.[5]

But Klein's conclusion overreaches the evidence. Although the
parable's main point is human accountability to God and not
God's sovereignty, Jesus does not base the reason for God's election on acceptance of the invitation, as Klein understands it.
Jesus does not say that some are elect *because* they accepted the
invitation. He merely ends by saying, "For many are called, but

---

4. Robert H. Gundry, *Matthew: A Commentary on His Literary and Theological Art*
(Grand Rapids: Eerdmans, 1982), 441. Cf. Morris, *Matthew*, 552.
5. Klein, *The New Chosen People*, 67–69 (italics in original).

few are chosen" (Matt. 22:14). Jesus does not indicate why some are chosen. He does not here say that election is based on either God's sovereign love or foreseen faith. It is inappropriate, then, to seek to derive the basis of election from this parable.

Conclusion. The doctrine of election is developed from the Old Testament to the gospels. As Grant Osborne explains, "The election motif is an important element in the theology of Jesus and transforms the corporate identity of Israel's view to the individual thrust of Jesus' view."[6] That statement is generally correct as long as we keep in mind that there were instances of individual election in the Old Testament, and that New Testament election is both individual and corporate.

Furthermore, Jesus teaches that God chose certain Israelites and Gentiles for salvation. God will protect them during the difficult times ahead and will guard them from spiritual deception, and the returning Christ will usher them into his kingdom.

The Election of Jesus

In at least three places, the Synoptic Gospels teach that Jesus was chosen by God to perform his roles as servant, Son, and Messiah.

Matthew 12:18. Matthew's gospel records Jesus' healing of a man with a withered hand amid opposition from Jewish leaders concerning Sabbath-keeping (Matt. 12:9–13). After Jesus heals the man's hand, the Pharisees conspire to destroy him. Knowing their evil intentions, he withdraws, many of the people follow him, and he heals many. Then Jesus commands "them not to make him known" (v. 16), and thereby fulfills Isaiah's prophecy:

> Behold, my servant whom I have chosen, my beloved with whom my soul is well pleased. I will put my Spirit upon him, and he

6. Grant Osborne, "Exegetical Notes on Calvinist Texts," in *Grace Unlimited*, ed. Clark H. Pinnock (Minneapolis: Bethany House, 1975), 168.

will proclaim justice to the Gentiles. He will not quarrel or cry aloud, nor will anyone hear his voice in the streets; a bruised reed he will not break, and a smoldering wick he will not quench, until he brings justice to victory; and in his name the Gentiles will hope. (Matt. 12:18–21, quoting Isa. 42:1–3)

Jesus fulfills Isaiah 42:1–3 in his earthly ministry when, preaching and healing by the power of the Spirit, he instructs his audience not to publicize his ministry. In this way, he did "not quarrel or cry aloud." His desire to be unnoticed before the time fulfills Isaiah's words: "a bruised reed he will not break, and a smoldering wick he will not quench." Matthew's message is plain: Jesus is identifiable as the servant of the Lord whom God *chose*.

Luke 9:35. Jesus, praying on the mountain with Peter, James, and John, is transfigured so that "the appearance of his face" is "altered, and his clothing" becomes "dazzling white" (Luke 9:29). After Moses and Elijah appear in glory on the mountain and Peter foolishly proposes to make three tents, one each for Jesus, Moses, and Elijah, God intervenes. A cloud of the divine presence overshadows them, and God speaks: "This is my Son, my *Chosen One*; listen to him!" (v. 35)—at which point the three disciples see only Jesus with them.

Here again we learn that Jesus is chosen by God to perform certain roles. One of these roles is hinted at by what Moses and Elijah (representing the Law and the Prophets) discuss with Jesus—"his departure, which he was about to accomplish at Jerusalem" (v. 31). The Greek word used here for "departure" is *exodus*. Because Moses, who led the Old Testament exodus, is discussing Jesus' *exodus* with him, the word not only refers to Jesus' departure from this world (i.e., his death) but also typologically corresponds to this great redemptive event of the Old Testament. Jesus' death is the New Testament *exodus* that will redeem all who believe in Christ.

Not only is Jesus chosen by God to be the Redeemer; he is also the Prophet, as indicated by the Father's words in verse 35, "Listen to him!" These words are an echo of Deuteronomy 18:15, where

God promises to send Israel a prophet like Moses and says: "It is to him you shall listen." Peter, James, and John are to listen to Jesus, who was chosen by God to be the Redeemer and great Prophet.

Luke 23:35. Luke uniquely records the scoffing of the Jewish rulers at the foot of Jesus' cross: "He saved others; let him save himself, if he is the Christ of God, his *Chosen One!*" (Luke 23:35). Ironically, these rulers speak for God when they mockingly call the crucified Jesus God's "Chosen One." So he was. As the God-man, he was chosen to die on the cross for sinners, including both Jews and Gentiles. (Luke later indicates that many Jewish leaders were saved. See Acts 6:7.)

Conclusion. Although they occur outside the Synoptics, Peter's words also indicate that Jesus was chosen by God to perform a mission: "[Christ] was foreknown before the foundation of the world . . . , a living stone rejected by men but in the sight of God *chosen* and precious" (1 Peter 1:20; 2:4). What is the significance of the fact that four New Testament passages teach that Jesus was chosen by God?

Jesus' election pertains to his humanity and mission. God the Father chose the incarnate Son to be the servant of the Lord spoken of in Isaiah 42:1 (Matt. 12:18). He chose him as the God-*man* to be Redeemer (Luke 9:31; 23:35) and Prophet (Luke 9:31). The Father chose Christ as a human being to be Redeemer of the world. John Calvin, following Augustine, presents the election of Christ as a man as evidence for the unconditional election of individuals:

> By what virtues will they say that he deserved in the womb itself to be made head of the angels, only-begotten Son of God, image and glory of the Father, light, righteousness, and salvation of the world . . . But if they willfully strive to strip God of his free power to choose or reject, let them at the same time also take away what has been given to Christ.[7]

7. John Calvin, *Institutes of the Christian Religion* 3:22:1, ed. John T. McNeill (Philadelphia: Westminster Press, 1960), 933.

Plainly, Christ's election does not pertain to his eternal relations with the Father and Holy Spirit before the creation of the world; it has to do with his becoming one of us to be our Redeemer. It pertains to him as a human being, specifically as our divine-*human* Deliverer. But the question must be asked: does viewing Christ as elect demean him? That the answer to this question is negative is evident when we compare Christ's election with ours. Christ's election is unlike ours in that we were chosen as sinners for redemption but he as the Sinless One to be our Redeemer. Paul Jewett hits the nail on the head: "It is not what we are *delivered from* but what we are *elected to* that is the element common to the election of Christ and his people. As we are elected to life, so is Christ our Lord, who triumphed over death in the resurrection . . . We are chosen in him, not he in us."[8]

Election in the Gospel of John

The fourth gospel says more about election than the first three. John paints two pictures that describe God's election of his people: the Father's giving people to the Son and the prior identity of that people. These pictures occur in three passages: John 6:35–45; 10:26–30; 17:2, 6, 9–10, 24. In addition, in one passage John presents Jesus as the author of election (15:14–19).

The Election of the People of God

John 6:35–45. After multiplying the loaves and fish (vv. 1–15), Jesus delivers his famous Bread of Life Discourse (vv. 25–59). He is the living bread who eternally satisfies the spiritual appetite of believers. He blames the Jews for seeing him but not believing (v. 36). By contrast, he then says, "All that the Father gives me will come to me" (v. 37). The meaning of "coming" to Jesus is given in verse 35: "I am the bread of life; whoever *comes* to me shall not

8. Paul Jewett, *Election and Predestination* (Grand Rapids: Eerdmans, 1985), 55 (italics in original).

hunger, and whoever *believes* in me shall never thirst." "Coming" to Jesus means believing in him. Jesus teaches, therefore, that all whom the Father gives him will believe in him.

The Father's giving people to Jesus is a picture of election. It is critical to understand that the Father's giving people to the Son precedes their believing in him for salvation. "All that the Father gives me *will come* to me" (John 6:37). The future tense of the verb "come" indicates that the Father's giving people to the Son infallibly results in their believing in Jesus. That is, election precedes faith and results in faith. For this reason, it is incorrect to maintain that election is based on God's foreseeing people's faith. Moreover, the Son will keep those same people for final salvation: "And this is the will of him who sent me, that I should lose nothing of all that he has given me, but raise it up on the last day" (v. 39). In Jesus' Bread of Life Discourse, then, he speaks twice of the Father's giving people to him. Each time, he points to the Father's election of many people to believe in the Son and gain eternal life.

Arminian biblical scholars reach a very different conclusion concerning this passage. Listen to I. Howard Marshall, Grant Osborne, and Norman Geisler, respectively:

> The men whom the Father gives to Jesus are those Jews who have already responded to Him.

> The sovereign force considers human responsibility before moving.

> Their being drawn by God was conditioned on their faith . . . Their understanding of Jesus' teaching and being drawn to the Father resulted from their own *free choice.*[9]

On what do these authors base this conclusion? They appeal to places in John's gospel, in both the immediate and wider contexts of John 6, that speak of the necessity of people's believing

---

9. Marshall, *Kept by the Power of God*, 178; Osborne, "Exegetical Notes on Calvinist Texts," 171; Norman Geisler, *Chosen but Free: A Balanced View of Divine Election*, 2nd ed. (Minneapolis: Bethany House, 2001), 93 (italics in original).

in Christ for salvation (John 3:16–18; 6:37, 40) and of God's finding people guilty for not believing (John 1:11; 5:38; 6:36).

Before addressing the Arminian appeal to John's theme of
human responsibility, it is necessary to examine John 6:45: "It
is written in the Prophets, 'And they will all be taught by God.'
Everyone who has heard and learned from the Father comes to
me." Marshall and Klein both interpret this as teaching human
freedom in salvation, a freedom that they regard as incompatible with a Calvinistic understanding of John 6:37.[10] But these
esteemed scholars have both misunderstood John 6:37. Jesus
does not here emphasize human responsibility but divine sovereignty. Jesus' use of Isaiah 54:13—"They will all be taught by
God"—points to God's sovereign, inward, and effective teaching
his people of the things of God. Such an understanding clarifies
the next words: "Everyone who has heard and learned from the
Father comes to me," that is, those inwardly and efficaciously
taught by the Father believe in Jesus. Instead of affirming human
freedom, John 6:37 underscores the powerful and mysterious
working of God in the hearts of his people, all of whom will be
"taught by God." John 6:45, then, reaffirms the truth of 6:37: "All
that the Father gives me will come to me."

I agree with my Arminian brothers and sisters that frequently
in John's gospel Jesus invites sinners to believe in him for salvation, including John 6:35, 40. I also agree that in numerous
verses, including John 6:36 and 6:64, Jesus condemns sinners
for not believing in him. But neither of those facts determines
in advance how we should interpret John 6:37. It is improper
theological method to bend verses to fit our theology. When Jesus
says, "All that the Father gives me will come to me," he teaches
that the Father's "giving" precedes sinners' "coming" to him. In
other words, predestination precedes faith. I do not fully understand how God can be absolutely sovereign and sinners fully
responsible, but I am convinced that the Bible teaches that both
concepts are true. In short, John teaches that Jesus invites sinners

10. Marshall, *Kept by the Power of God*, 176; Klein, *The New Chosen People*, 143.

to come to him, but he condemns them for rejecting him. And at the same time he teaches in John 6:37 that God's sovereignty precedes and enables their believing.

John 10:26–30. Jesus is the Good Shepherd who voluntarily gives his life for the sheep and raises himself from the dead (vv. 11, 17–18). Although his messages and miracles loudly testify to his identity, many of his hearers spurn him. Jesus provides a behind-the-scenes explanation: On the one hand, "You do not believe because you are not part of my flock." On the other hand, "My sheep hear my voice, and I know them, and they follow me" (vv. 26–27).

Jesus separates his hearers into the two categories of (1) sheep and (2) those who are not sheep (I will call them "goats"). Notice that all people fit into one of these two categories: they are either sheep or goats. Furthermore, Jesus implies that his hearers are either sheep or goats *before* they respond to him. Indeed, their response of faith or unbelief does not *make* them either sheep or goats. Rather, their responses *show* their prior identities. Listen carefully to Jesus' words: "But you do not believe because you are not part of my flock. My sheep hear my voice" (vv. 26–27).

Contrary to a common misunderstanding, Jesus does not say that they are goats because they do not believe, but rather that they do not believe because they are goats. Jesus therefore teaches God's election of human beings for salvation. People are sheep or goats before they believe in or reject Jesus. Their belief or unbelief reveals their prior identities.

Once again it is important to preserve a sense of balance. Jesus' strong teaching on divine predestination given here is not the only message, or even the main one, of the gospel of John. More often Jesus speaks of human freedom. In the same chapter in which Jesus teaches about the prior identities of the sheep and the goats—John 10—he also condemns unbelieving hearers for their lack of faith (v. 25) and invites people to believe in him (vv. 37–38). Later, in chapter 8 on free will, we will explore the relation between God's sovereignty and human freedom. For now, we note that the fourth gospel teaches both.

John 17:2, 6, 9–10, 24. In his High Priestly Prayer, Jesus prays to the Father in anticipation of the cross, empty tomb, and return to heaven. Throughout the prayer, we learn that the Son's mission of salvation is controlled by the Father's prior election of people for salvation. Although the Father "ha[s] given" the Son "authority over all flesh," the Son gives "eternal life [only] to all whom" the Father has "given him" (17:2). This means that the Son rules over all human beings, but gives the gift of eternal life only to the elect. Jesus proceeds to explain his mission: "I have manifested your name to the people whom you gave me out of the world" (v. 6). Consequently, all those whom the Father gave to the Son receive the divine message and believe in the Son (vv. 7–8).

Jesus' prayers likewise reflect a prior divine discrimination. "I am praying for them. I am not praying for the world but for those whom you have given me, for they are yours" (v. 9). Here Jesus uses the word "world" to refer to those not given to him by the Father. They are not the object of his prayer; rather, he prays only for the elect.

Envisioning his death and resurrection as already accomplished, Jesus asks the Father to bring the chosen to join Jesus in heaven: "Father, I desire that they also, whom you have given me, may be with me where I am, to see my glory that you have given me because you loved me before the foundation of the world" (v. 24). Once again Jesus prays only for the salvation of the ones whom the Father gave him, that is, the elect.

In sum: in this justly famous passage, John portrays those chosen for salvation as the gift of the Father to his Son. They first belonged to the Father, and he gave them to Jesus (17:6). Jesus gives eternal life and reveals the Father to them alone; he prays for them alone, and asks the Father to take them to heaven (17:2, 6, 9–10, 24). D. A. Carson draws out an important implication: "The giving by the Father of certain men to the Son precedes their reception of eternal life, and governs the purpose of the Son's mission. There is no way to escape the implicit election."[11]

Nevertheless, well-intentioned Arminian scholars try to escape the implicit election in John 17. William Klein, for example, writes:

> As we saw in 6:37–40, both with *give* and God's *will*, faith in Jesus is the key to eternal life. Here Jesus gives no warrant to read in some pretemporal idea of predestination. In the context of John's gospel, the "given ones" are believers, in contrast to the unbelieving world out of which they have come.[12]

Although much of what Klein says is accurate, it does not pertain to the Father's giving people to the Son in John 17. Of course faith in Jesus is the key to eternal life. But that is not the issue at hand. The issue is the connection between people's being "given" to Christ and their believing in him. It is also true that John 17 does not locate the "giving" before creation, as Paul does. But that fact, too, does not directly bear on the meaning of the "giving."

When Klein says that the "given ones" are believers, he errs. He reverses the order of John 17. Not once does Jesus teach that the Father gave people to him because they believe in him, because he foresaw their faith, or the like. Rather, the Father's giving a people to Jesus precedes their receiving eternal life (v. 2). And Jesus does not manifest the Father to people because they believe in him. Instead, he manifests the Father to the people whom the Father gave him, and as a result they receive Jesus' words and believe that the Father sent him (vv. 6–8). That is, the Father does not give them to the Son because they believe, but they believe because the Father gave them to his Son.[13]

---

11. D. A. Carson, *Divine Sovereignty and Human Responsibility: Biblical Perspectives in Tension* (Grand Rapids: Baker, 1994), 187.

12. Klein, *The New Chosen People*, 142.

13. See Robert W. Yarbrough, "Divine Election in the Gospel of John," in *Still Sovereign: Contemporary Perspectives on Election, Foreknowledge, and Grace*, ed. Thomas R. Schreiner and Bruce A. Ware (Grand Rapids: Baker, 2000), 56–62, for strong argumentation that divine election is the cause of faith.

Jesus as the Author of Election

John 15:14–19. Jesus uses the analogy of the vine and the branches to instruct his disciples in the importance of fruit-bearing. Then he gives them assurance that they are no longer slaves but his friends, if they obey him. Next he teaches his eleven disciples (Judas has already gone out to betray him), "You did not choose me, but I chose you and appointed you that you should go and bear" enduring fruit (vv. 14–16). Jesus implies that the fruitful branches of whom he previously spoke are those he has chosen. They are fruitful because he chose and appointed them to bear fruit.

Some maintain that John 15:16 speaks of Jesus' choice of people for service and discipleship rather than for eternal life:

> The purpose for the election was mission. . . . This is clearly appointment for ministry. . . . This is election of individuals to a task.[14]

> The point is that this election had nothing to do with whether a person went to heaven or to hell; it was the bestowal of an office and a task.[15]

Indeed, Jesus tells of just such a choice in John 6:70: "Did I not choose you, the Twelve? And yet one of you is a devil." But Jesus' choosing of the Eleven in John 15:16 is not the same as his choosing of the Twelve in 6:70. In John 15:16, Jesus issues a warning to the disciples that the world will hate them since it hated him first. He then clarifies: "If you were of the world, the world would love you as its own; but because you are not of the world, but I chose you out of the world, therefore the world hates you" (15:19).

Jesus' choice in John 6:70 was a choice of twelve to be his disciples. His choice in 15:16, 19 is a choice of the eleven disciples "out of the world" that results in their no longer belonging to the world, but henceforth to Jesus. Furthermore, John 6:70 is not

---

14. Klein, *The New Chosen People*, 132.

15. Roger T. Forster and V. Paul Marston, *God's Strategy in Human History* (Wheaton, IL: Tyndale House, 1973), 120.

parallel to John 15:16, but it is parallel to John 13:18 where, after washing his disciples' feet, Jesus says, "I am not speaking to all of you; I know whom I have chosen." Just before, Jesus had said, "'And you are clean, but not every one of you.' For he knew who was to betray him; that was why he said, 'Not all of you are clean'" (John 13:10–11). Judas, therefore, was chosen to be one of the Twelve (6:70), but was not chosen for salvation (13:10–11; 15:16, 19). This is confirmed by the fact that Judas exits at the end of John 13 to betray the Master and is therefore not present in chapter 15. Using previously introduced terminology, then, we can say that Judas was historically elected but not eternally elected.

D. A. Carson displays the balance that is needed in treating God's supremacy and human responsibility:

> The disciples cannot even legitimately boast that they are believers on the ground that they, unlike others, wisely made the right choice. On the contrary: Jesus chose them. Merit theology is thus totally savaged. On the other hand, that Jesus chose them does not entail a robot-like stance on the part of the disciples, but increased responsibility—responsibility to produce enduring fruit (15:16), to pray (15:16b), to love each other (15:17). Election entails both privilege and responsibility.[16]

One other matter deserves attention. Despite the Arminian claim that God chooses people for service and not for salvation, this passage shows that both concepts are true. Jesus chose eleven men so that they would no longer belong to the world but to him; that is, he chose them for salvation (John 15:19). He also chose them so that they would bear lasting fruit; that is, he chose them for service (v. 16). Salvation and service are compatible.

Conclusion

It is time to draw some conclusions concerning election in John's gospel. The following three themes have relevance to the

---

16. Carson, *Divine Sovereignty and Human Responsibility*, 191.

doctrine of predestination: the Father's giving people to Jesus, the fact that some are identified as the people of God prior to faith, and Jesus' choosing his disciples out of the world.

Arminian views of election have difficulty in light of the teaching of the fourth gospel. The idea that election is only corporate and not individual does not square with John's teaching. In John, as in the Old Testament, election is both individual and corporate. The Father and Son chose individuals to belong to them and to the people of God.

Similarly, the contention that election is for service and not salvation is a false choice because John's gospel specifically relates election to both salvation and service. For example, Jesus prays, "Father, I desire that they also, whom you have given me, may be with me where I am, to see my glory" (17:24). Jesus prays that the elect might be brought to heaven, that is, final salvation. And again, Jesus prays, "Father, the hour has come; glorify your Son that the Son may glorify you, since you have given him authority over all flesh, to give eternal life to all whom you have given him" (John 17:1–2; see also 6:37–40; 10:27–29; 15:19; 17:6, 9–10, 24). This is clearly predestination to eternal life. At the same time, election is for service, as John 15:16 makes plain: "You did not choose me, but I chose you and appointed you that you should go and bear" enduring fruit (vv. 14–16).

Furthermore, the fourth gospel does not verify the Arminian view that God chooses on the basis of foreseen faith. Indeed, because faith is the result of election, the basis of election resides in God's action and not in people's. To cite one example: Jesus said, "All that the Father gives me will come to me" (John 6:37; see also 10:27; 15:19; 17:2, 6, 9, 24). Predestination is not based on faith; faith is the result of the Father's prior election.

Election in the Acts of the Apostles

Luke emphasizes God's sovereignty both in his gospel and in Acts, as Arminian New Testament scholar I. Howard Marshall points out:

What Luke stresses is the supremacy of God over the world, especially in bringing salvation to mankind. . . . The situation is the same with regard to the early church. The early church saw that its own life was similarly under divine control, and ranged it alongside the ministry of Jesus as the sphere of God's activity. Throughout Acts the notes of divine fore-ordination and necessity are if anything stronger than in the Gospel. . . . The main feature of Luke's teaching about God thus lies in the thought of His plan, announced in the Old Testament and presently being fulfilled in history by His obedient servants.[17]

Calvinist New Testament scholar Donald Guthrie concludes: "It is not surprising in view of this strong emphasis on the divine choice that certain statements in Acts focus on predestination."[18] We will investigate two such statements, those of Acts 13:48 and 18:9–10.

Acts 13:48

Luke's account of the ministry of Paul and Barnabas in Pisidian Antioch on the first missionary journey resembles a roller-coaster ride. Their hearers alternately believe their message and persecute them. As a result, the apostles are up (13:42–44), down (vv. 45–46), up (vv. 47–49), and down (vv. 50–51). In the midst of the vacillating responses, the Gentiles turn to the Lord, when they hear Paul and Barnabas quote Isaiah 49:6: "I have made you a light for the Gentiles, that you may bring salvation to the ends of the earth" (Acts 13:47). Luke explains the reason for the Gentiles' conversion: "And when the Gentiles heard this, they began rejoicing and glorifying the word of the Lord, and as many as were appointed to eternal life believed" (v. 48).

Luke presents a divine classification or appointment to eternal life. And that appointment to eternal life precedes faith on

17. I. Howard Marshall, *Luke: Historian and Theologian* (Grand Rapids: Zondervan, 1970), 104, 106–7.
18. Donald Guthrie, *New Testament Theology* (Downers Grove, IL: InterVarsity Press, 1981), 618.

the part of the believers—"as many as were appointed to eternal life believed."

Arminians have employed at least four strategies in attempting to harmonize Acts 13:48 with their view of predestination. First, some have simply declared dogmatically, "Surely in this context Luke does not intend to restrict the application of salvation only to those appointed."[19] But to simply assume that one's position is correct on a matter under debate is to beg the question. Second, William G. MacDonald, aware that the word translated "appointed" could be rendered as a passive ("were appointed") or as a middle ("appointed themselves"), opts for the latter possibility and translates: *"and as many as were putting themselves in a position for eternal life believed."*[20] Notice the switch from "appointed themselves" to "were putting themselves in a position for eternal life." MacDonald claims that the Gentile believers in Pisidian Antioch ordained themselves for eternal life! It is not surprising, then, that other Arminian biblical scholars do not follow his lead. Third, Marshall reads into this passage the assumption that the Gentiles spoken of "were already proselytes and worshippers of God."[21] There is no evidence in the text for this; Marshall merely assumes mitigating circumstances to rescue his view. Fourth, Klein claims, "The Gentiles believed and entered the category of the appointed ones."[22] On the contrary, in this text there is a category of appointed ones (known only to God), and when Paul preached, appointed Gentiles believed the message. It is erroneous on the basis of this passage to claim that election is based on foreseen faith. Rather, faith is the result of God's prior election.

Acts 18:9-10

In Corinth on his second missionary journey, the apostle Paul has reason to be discouraged. He has testified to the Jews that

19. Klein, *The New Chosen People*, 110.
20. William G. MacDonald, "The Biblical Doctrine of Election," in *The Grace of God and the Will of Man*, ed. Clark Pinnock (Grand Rapids: Zondervan, 1989), 227 (italics in original).
21. Marshall, *Kept by the Power of God*, 84.
22. Klein, *The New Chosen People*, 121; cf. 109–110.

Jesus was the Christ, but they oppose him to the point of being abusive. He protests and announces that he is going to the Gentiles (Acts 18:5–6). Paul, who has been evangelizing in the synagogue, moves next door and has a fruitful ministry (vv. 7–8).

The Lord speaks to Paul in a vision one night to strengthen him. He tells him to continue preaching the gospel (v. 9). He promises to be with him and to protect him from harm. The Lord assures the apostle, "I have many in this city who are my people" (v. 10). Paul obediently stays on in Corinth for eighteen months ministering the Word of God (v. 11).

Luke declares that some Corinthians belonged to God even before they believed the gospel. F. F. Bruce agrees: "The Lord had many people in Corinth whom He had marked out for His own."[23] How have Arminian scholars dealt with this passage? They have read into the text the idea that God "had many people" based on his foreknowledge of their accepting the gospel. Listen to Marshall:

> "I am with you . . . I have many people in this city." The "many people" are usually and rightly regarded as people who would form Paul's field for evangelism and not as the many who had already believed (Acts 18:8). Hence the forces of evil would not prevent Paul from accomplishing the work given to him by God. Divine foreknowledge is accordingly taught in this verse, but it is not necessary to assume that a rigid predestination is present also.[24]

It is true that the "many . . . people" referred to in Acts 18:10 had not yet believed. But the text says nothing about God's foreseeing their faith. Rather, God reveals to Paul that many people in Corinth belonged to God even before they believed in order to embolden Paul to keep preaching the gospel there in difficult circumstances. Of course, they had not yet believed—but God had claimed them in advance by his grace; and when Paul preached to them, they would believe. Interestingly, God's telling Paul that

23. F. F. Bruce, *The Book of the Acts*, New International Commentary on the New Testament (Grand Rapids: Eerdmans, 1988), 372.

24. Marshall, *Kept by the Power of God*, 85. Cf. Osborne, "Exegetical Notes on Calvinist Texts," 175.

he has marked out people for salvation strengthens the apostle for ministry. Although some claim that an emphasis on God's sovereignty in salvation hinders evangelism, that emphasis had the opposite effect on Paul—it encouraged the apostle to continue preaching.

Conclusion

Given the strong emphases on God's sovereignty and preaching in Acts, we are not surprised to find material pertaining to election. At least two passages indicate a divine choice to salvation. Contrary to the Arminian notion that election is only corporate and not individual, in Acts it is both. Acts 13:48 and 18:9–10 teach that God chose individuals for salvation. These individuals, of course, make up the church.

In addition, the Arminian idea that election is for service and not salvation collides with Acts 13:48: "as many as were appointed to eternal life believed." Luke here teaches that individual predestination is unto eternal life. Once more I opt for "both/and" rather than "either/or." Those chosen for eternal life believe the gospel and are to serve the Lord. Election thus results in both salvation and service.

Acts does not give the basis of election, but the Arminian idea of election based on God's foreseeing faith clashes with Acts 13:48, where faith is the consequence (not the cause) of election. Predestination is not based on what human beings do, but is hidden in God.

Luke helpfully shows that God's election of people for salvation serves to strengthen Paul's apostolic preaching ministry. William J. Larkin comments on Acts 18:9–10: "The Lord's predestination (13:48) not only guarantees a fruitful preaching ministry but demands that Paul responsibly fulfill his obligation to witness."[25]

---

25. William J. Larkin Jr., *Acts*, InterVarsity Press New Testament Commentary (Downers Grove, IL: InterVarsity Press, 1995), 265.

Election in the General Epistles and Revelation

Having surveyed the Bible's teaching on election in the Old Testament, the Gospels, and Acts, we now turn our attention to the New Testament epistles and Revelation. Because Paul is the Bible's major teacher of predestination, we will save his epistles for last. First, we will survey the General Epistles and Revelation.

- The General Epistles
  - The Election of the People of God
  - The Election of Christ

- Revelation
  - Revelation 17:14
  - The Book of Life

The General Epistles

The Election of the People of God

James 2:5. James condemns the sin of partiality in his readers: "My brothers, show no partiality as you hold the faith in our Lord Jesus Christ, the Lord of glory" (James 2:1). Specifically, James's readers were paying special attention to the wealthy and neglecting the poor (vv. 2–3). When they act like this, James insists, they "become judges with evil thoughts" (v. 4). In so doing, they do not act as people made in the image of God, for he shows favor to the poor: "Listen, my beloved brothers, has not God *chosen* those who are poor in the world to be rich in faith and heirs of the kingdom, which he has promised to those who love him?" (v. 5). Here alone in his epistle James speaks to the topic of predestination. Of course, God also chooses rich people for salvation. But James focuses on God's election of the poor because this shows that God honors the poor, the very thing that James's readers were not doing (v. 6).

William Klein rejects the view that I have set forth—that James 2:5 speaks of God's election of people to salvation. Why?

> Unquestionably, God has not chosen *all* the poor, for many reject the gospel. And clearly God has chosen *some* rich. To hold a meaning for *eklegomai* (choose) that requires such qualifications evacuates the phrase "God chose the poor" of its meaning.[1]

But the text does not say that God chose *all* the poor or that he excluded the rich, only that he has chosen poor people. Unlike James's readers, who reject the poor, God includes poor people (along with many others) in his election to salvation.

Klein espouses that James 2:5 is "a proverbial expression," and he paraphrases it: "Has not God chosen the poor in spirit, those willing to obey me and depend on me rather than on their own resources (as the rich do)?" In this way, Klein reads historical election into a text that speaks of election to salvation. I say this because James specifies the goal of election: God elected many poor persons "to be rich in faith and heirs of the kingdom" of God. Klein also reads conditional election (based on foreseen works?) into James 2:5 when the text says nothing about the basis of God's choice.

1 Peter 1:1–2. Peter addresses his first epistle thus: "To those who are elect exiles of the dispersion in Pontus, Galatia,

---

1. William W. Klein, *The New Chosen People: A Corporate View of Election* (Grand Rapids: Academie Books, 1990), 226 (italics in original).

Cappadocia, Asia, and Bithynia, according to the foreknowledge of God the Father, in the sanctification of the Spirit, for obedience to Jesus Christ and for sprinkling with his blood." Peter describes believers as chosen by God and as pilgrims in five Roman provinces. He depicts salvation in terms of the Trinity—Christians are chosen for salvation according to the *Father's* foreknowledge, set apart by the *Spirit*, resulting in obedience to the gospel and cleansing by *Christ's* sacrificial death. I. Howard Marshall aptly summarizes Peter's emphasis:

> First Peter . . . lays considerable emphasis upon the great power and grace of God in caring for His people even in the midst of persecution. Thus it is addressed to those who are the elect sojourners of the dispersion, elect according to God's foreknowledge (1 Peter 1:1f.). These words imply that God's gracious choice rested upon the readers before they were aware of it, His aim being to produce in them obedience and consecration.[2]

Evangelicals agree with Marshall's summary, but they divide over the meaning of God's foreknowledge in the context of his choosing people for salvation based on that foreknowledge.[3] Arminians say that God chooses those whom he knows in advance will believe the gospel. Calvinists say that God chooses those whom he specially loves in advance. Because it is impossible to resolve that debate based on this passage, we will return to the debate when we consider Romans 8:28–30.

1 Peter 2:9. Peter describes the Jewish and Gentile Christians to whom he writes in terms of Old Testament designations for Israel: "But you are a chosen race, a royal priesthood, a holy nation, a people for his own possession, that you may proclaim the excellencies of him who called you out of darkness into his marvelous

---

2. I. Howard Marshall, *Kept by the Power of God: A Study of Perseverance and Falling Away* (London: Epworth Press, 1969), 157.

3. Klein is mistaken, therefore, when he writes concerning this passage: "Peter does not base God's choice of some to be Christians on his foreknowledge . . ." *The New Chosen People*, 240.

light." Peter means that the Christian church is the new Israel, the new covenant people of God. Peter uses "a chosen race," one of those designations, containing language from Deuteronomy 10:15 and Isaiah 43:20, to describe the church as chosen by God to belong to him. Peter here teaches God's corporate election of the church to be his people. Both God's choice of the church and its resultant status are in view—the church is special because God chose it.[4]

1 Peter 5:13. In the final greetings of his first epistle, Peter writes: "She who is at Babylon, who is likewise *chosen*, sends you greetings, and so does Mark, my son." Although some earlier commentators understood "she who is at Babylon" to refer to Peter's wife or a famous woman in Rome, almost certainly it refers to a church as chosen by God.[5] This is, therefore, a reference to God's corporate election of the church.

2 Peter 1:10. Peter has already urged his readers to cultivate Christian virtues in order to be effective and productive for God (2 Peter 1:5–8). If believers are growing in these virtues, their confidence of salvation will grow. Now Peter urges: "Therefore, brothers, be all the more diligent to make your calling and election sure" (v. 10). By "calling" Peter refers to God's effectively summoning people to salvation through faith in Jesus Christ. Here as elsewhere Scripture connects predestination and calling.

And those whom he predestined he also called. (Rom. 8:30)

God . . . has endured with much patience . . . in order to make known the riches of his glory for vessels of mercy, which he has

---

4. Klein errs when he downplays God's choice of the church in order to highlight its chosen status, for both are in view. *The New Chosen People*, 244.
5. "While some older commentators have argued that 'she' was Peter's wife, who did apparently travel with him (1 Cor. 9:5; cf. Matt. 8:14), it is highly unlikely that he would not have named her had she been well enough known to the Christians in Asia Minor to send greetings, nor is it likely that she rather than Peter would be linked to 'Babylon.' Rather, as is the case in 2 John 1, 13, the 'lady' in question is 'Ekklesia,' the church." Peter H. Davids, *The First Epistle of Peter*, New International Commentary on the New Testament (Grand Rapids: Eerdmans, 1990), 201.

prepared beforehand for glory—even us whom he has called. (Rom. 9:22–24)

Peter puts calling before election because people learn that God has chosen them when he calls them to salvation. We do not learn of our predestination by searching God's eternal counsels, but by believing in Christ, as 1 Thessalonians 1:4–5 teaches as well.

Why does Peter exhort his readers to make their election sure? Not because it is uncertain to God, for he knows whom he has chosen. Rather, Peter exhorts them to make certain their election for themselves. How do they accomplish this? Although the full answer of Scripture is more complicated, the partial answer given here is that believers personally gain assurance of God's choosing and calling them to salvation as they grow in Christian virtues. When they observe God building their character to be more like Christ's, they are strengthened in their conviction that God has summoned them to faith in Christ and chosen them for salvation. As Peter Davids explains, "What about those who are concerned that they might not be truly elect? Their lifestyle of obedience to Christ, which flows from trust in him, should be convincing proof of their state of grace."[6]

2 John 1, 13. At the beginning and end of his second epistle, John speaks of churches as chosen by God.

The elder to the elect lady and her children, whom I love in truth . . . (2 John 1)

The children of your elect sister greet you. (2 John 13)

Although it is possible that in verse 1 John refers to a woman by name ("Electa" or "Kyria") or to a woman by a title of honor ("elect Lady"), it is most likely that he refers to a church

6. Walter C. Kaiser Jr., Peter H. Davids, F. F. Bruce, and Manfred T. Brauch, *Hard Sayings of the Bible* (Downers Grove, IL: InterVarsity Press, 1996), 726.

in verses 1 and 13. As Peter Davids notes, this is because "the switch in Greek to the second person plural in 2 John 8, 10 and 12 (before returning to the second person singular in 2 John 13) appears to indicate that the elder has a group in mind, not an individual."[7] Similarly to Peter (in 1 Peter 5:13), then, John in these two instances speaks of Christian churches as elected by God for salvation. Here again we find a corporate view of election.

The Election of Christ

Two passages in 1 Peter speak of Christ's election as Savior.

1 Peter 1:20. Peter seeks to motivate believers to live holy and reverent lives for God by reminding them of the cost of their deliverance:

> Conduct yourselves with fear throughout the time of your exile, knowing that you were ransomed from the futile ways inherited from your forefathers, not with perishable things such as silver or gold, but with the precious blood of Christ, like that of a lamb without blemish or spot. He was foreknown before the foundation of the world but was made manifest in the last times for your sake, who through him are believers in God. (1 Peter 1:17–21)

Peter here contrasts his readers' redemption with that of the Old Testament Israelites. When God visited the final plague on the Egyptians, he passed over the firstborn males of Israel and thereby claimed them for himself. Later he took the tribe of Levi in place of the firstborn. But the number of Levites fell short of the number of firstborn by 273, and the shortfall had to be redeemed at the price of five shekels per head (Num. 3:40–51). By contrast, Peter's readers were redeemed with something much

7. Ibid., 745.

more precious than silver or gold—the blood of Christ, the spotless Lamb of God (cf. John 1:29).

Peter contrasts Christ's being foreknown and revealed: "He was foreknown before the foundation of the world but was made manifest in the last times for your sake" (1 Peter 1:20). Calvinists and Arminians debate the meaning of the words "foreknow" and "foreknowledge" with reference to God's choice of Christians. We will postpone discussion of that issue, because in view here is God's foreknowing of Christ, not of Christians.

What did Peter mean when he said that Christ "was foreknown"? Thomas Schreiner answers correctly: "Peter was not merely saying that God foresaw when Christ would come, though that is part of his meaning. He was also saying that God foreordained when Christ would come."[8] Although some Arminian scholars disagree with this conclusion, claiming that Peter's emphasis is on "prior *knowledge* more than prior determination,"[9] the context favors the former interpretation. Peter sets up a double contrast: between "was foreknown" and "was made manifest" and between "before the foundation of the world" and "in the last times." It would be trivial and unnecessary for Peter to say merely that God knew Christ before creation; of course he did. Peter Davids's explanation is worthy of quotation: "The emphasis in this passage is not merely on God's knowing about Jesus (prediction), but on his volition, which while long planned only now has come to fruition."[10]

It is important not to lose sight of the purpose for which Christ was chosen. He "was made manifest in the last times for your sake, who through him are believers in God, who raised him from the dead and gave him glory, so that your faith and hope are in God" (1 Peter 1:20–21). God chose Christ before creation,

---

8. Thomas R. Schreiner, *1, 2 Peter, Jude*, The New American Commentary (Nashville: Broadman & Holman, 2003), 53–54.

9. Klein, *The New Chosen People*, 235 (italics in original).

10. Davids, *The First Epistle of Peter*, 74 n. 9.

he designated him, to be the Redeemer of all those who would believe in him for eternal life.[11]

1 Peter 2:4, 6. Using Old Testament imagery, Peter speaks of the believers to whom he writes as priests and a living temple in which God is worshiped:

> As you come to him, a living stone rejected by men but in the sight of God chosen and precious, you yourselves like living stones are being built up as a spiritual house, to be a holy priesthood, to offer spiritual sacrifices acceptable to God through Jesus Christ. (1 Peter 2:4–5)

In so doing, Peter speaks of Christ as "a living stone . . . chosen and precious." This language is from Isaiah 28:16 in the Greek Old Testament, the Septuagint, which Peter adapts in 1 Peter 2:6: "Behold, I am laying in Zion a stone, a cornerstone chosen and precious, and whoever believes in him will not be put to shame." Jesus Christ is the essential and unavoidable foundation of the spiritual temple, the people of God. When the covenant nation of Israel rejects him, they fall against "a stone of stumbling, and a rock of offense" (v. 8), and as a result are condemned. But any Jews or Gentiles who build their lives on the foundation of Jesus Christ "will not be put to shame" (v. 6).

Peter, using Old Testament imagery of the Messiah as the cornerstone of the people of God, teaches that Christ is a "chosen and precious" living stone. Peter thereby depicts Christ as the chosen Savior of God's people, the one in whom people believe and whom they honor (vv. 6–7). Those who reject him will be put to shame, but "the honor is for you who believe" (v. 7).

Conclusion. Both of these Petrine passages (1:20; 2:4, 6), which portray Christ as foreknown Lamb and chosen stone,

---

11. J. Ramsey Michaels, *1 Peter,* vol. 49 of Word Biblical Commentary (Waco, TX: Word, 1988), 66.

respectively, present Christ as chosen by God to be the Redeemer of his people.

Revelation

Revelation contributes to our understanding of election by speaking of Christ's followers as chosen (in 17:14) and by painting the picture of the book of life.

Revelation 17:14

John predicts war between the Lamb and "ten kings" who align themselves with "the beast" and oppose God's kingdom (17:12–13). The outcome of this war is not in doubt: "They will make war on the Lamb, and the Lamb will conquer them, for he is Lord of lords and King of kings, and those with him are called and *chosen* and faithful" (17:14). The enemies of God fight against Christ and his saints, but the all-powerful Christ will defeat them. Christ's followers, who share in his victory, are described as "called and chosen and faithful." Here again we learn that God calls the people whom he has chosen; predestination and calling are linked. His people are further described as "faithful" because they refuse to worship the beast and remain committed to God.

The Book of Life

A theme from Revelation that pertains to the doctrine of election is that of "the book of life" (3:5; 17:8; 20:12, 15) or "the Lamb's book of life" (21:27; see also 13:8). This theme first occurs in the letter to the church in Sardis, where Jesus promises the one who perseveres, "I will never blot his name out of the book of life" (3:5). God will preserve those who conquer, and they will assuredly inherit eternal life with him.

That great enemy of God called "the beast" will exert tremendous power over much of humankind. In fact, "the dwellers on earth whose names have not been written in the book of life from the foundation of the world will marvel to see the beast" (17:8). Those whose names are not written in the book of life are left unprotected; to have one's name written there is to be protected by God from spiritual danger. Here, as in Ephesians 1:4 and 2 Timothy 1:9, God's choice of his people is "before the foundation of the world." God chose his people for salvation even before he created them.

The book of life serves as the census register of the city of God. The names of all those whom God has chosen appear there. The kings of the earth will "bring into" the New Jerusalem "the glory and the honor of the nations," and "nothing unclean will ever enter it . . . , but only those who are written in the Lamb's book of life" (Rev. 21:26–27).

By describing it as "the Lamb's book of life" (21:27) and "the book of life of the Lamb that was slain" (13:8), John indicates that the book belongs to Jesus by virtue of his having made atonement for the sins of his people. Perhaps this is why at the last judgment books are opened: books of deeds and the book of life. Judgment is based on human responsibility: "And the dead were judged by what was written in the books, according to what they had done" (20:12c). At the same time, the text sounds a note of divine sovereignty when it declares, "And if anyone's name was not found written in the book of life, he was thrown into the lake of fire" (20:15).

The chief way in which Arminians handle the theology of the book of life concerns Jesus' words, "I will never blot his name out of the book of life" (Rev. 3:5). Grant Osborne, for example, regards the book of life as a major motif in Revelation and affirms:

> Participation [in the book of life] depends on Christ's sacrificial death and the believer's faithful perseverance in Christ. Both aspects must remain intact. . . . The "book of life" itself contains both the names and deeds of all who claim allegiance to Christ, and only those who remain faithful will stay in it. The verb . . . I will blot out was often used of a name "erased" from a written record . . . and became a metaphor for removal or destruction.

Here those who remain "unspotted" from the pagan surroundings are promised eternal reward in the presence of God.[12]

Osborne interprets Jesus' saying that he will not blot people's names from the book of life as teaching that some will be blotted out, and then on that basis makes staying in the book dependent on human faithfulness. But Osborne misses the point of Revelation 3:5 in its context of the letters to the seven churches. Each letter promises final salvation to those who overcome. The promises are usually expressed in positive terms (2:7, 17, 26–28; 3:5, 12, 21), but three times in negative terms (2:11; 3:5, 12). It is important to see that both the positive and negative terms have the same purpose—to assure the overcomers of eternal bliss with God. So when Jesus says, "The one who conquers will not be hurt by the second death" (2:11), he means that they will surely enjoy eternal life. Similarly, when he says, "I will never blot his name out of the book of life" (3:5), he means that the one who overcomes will certainly be found in the book of life. He says nothing about names actually being blotted out of the book of life; rather, by employing "litotes," he underscores his promise. Litotes is the denial of a negative to make an emphatic positive statement. Thus, *never blotting out names* from the book means ensuring that those persons will be included. It is incorrect, therefore, to appeal to Revelation 3:5 to make the strong consolation offered by the passages concerning the book of life dependent on human reliability.

In fact, what is the chief use of the book of life in Revelation, taking all the passages into account? It is to assure those listed in the book of life of God's spiritual protection (3:5; 13:8; 17:8; 20:15; 21:27). Arminians sometimes claim that predestination does not result in salvation, but the passages mentioning the book of life disprove that claim because those written in the

---

12. Grant R. Osborne, *Revelation*, Baker Exegetical Commentary on the New Testament (Grand Rapids: Baker, 2002), 180–81. The idea that names can be erased from the book of life leads Klein to "doubt that this image conveys predestination or election. . . . The category 'those whose names . . . are written in the book' is simply another name for believers." *The New Chosen People*, 154.

book of life from creation (17:8) will be spared the lake of fire (20:15) and will enter the New Jerusalem (21:27).[13]

Conclusion

What does the study of the General Epistles and Revelation add to our understanding of election? First of all, 1 Peter 1:20 and 2:4, 6, like Isaiah 42:1, Matthew 12:18, and Luke 9:35 and 23:35, present Christ as chosen by God to be the Redeemer of his people.

Second, James reminds us that God has chosen human beings, even the poor, "to be rich in faith and heirs of the kingdom, which he has promised to those who love him" (James 2:5). That is, God has chosen people for salvation, including the poor. Peter adds that predestination is "according to the foreknowledge of God the Father" (1 Peter 1:2), a concept that we still need to study in detail. At present, we conclude that the Father foreknows and chooses his people. In addition, Peter urges his readers "to make" their "calling and election sure" for themselves (2 Peter 1:10) by cultivating Christian virtues. Revelation also combines calling and election when it refers to God's victorious followers as "called and chosen and faithful" (Rev. 17:14).

Third, Peter and John—in 1 Peter 2:9; 5:13; 2 John 1, 13—teach that God chose the church corporately to be his people. There is a corporate as well as an individual election. The book of Revelation combines individual and corporate predestination when it speaks of people's names being written in the book of life "from the foundation of the world" (17:8). This book records the names of those chosen for salvation because "only those who are written in the Lamb's book of life" will enter the eternal city of God (21:27). God will protect them from eternal death (3:5), worshiping the beast (13:8), the beast's deceptions (17:8), and the lake of fire (20:15). In other words, God will deliver his chosen ones from shame, deception, and hell, and guide them safely into the eternal city (21:27).

13. G. K. Beale, *The Book of Revelation: A Commentary on the Greek Text*, New International Greek Testament Commentary (Grand Rapids: Eerdmans, 1999), 281–82.

Election in Paul's Epistles, Part 1

When we think about the topic of election, our minds naturally fasten upon the writings of the apostle Paul. Paul's teaching about election has inspired and challenged all who have striven to understand this issue. To attempt to explain the theology of election requires that we zero in on what Paul wrote about the topic. Paul employs election concepts and terminology more than any other New Testament writer.[1]

William Klein is correct—Paul is the main theologian of election in the New Testament. Actually, he is the main theologian of election in the whole Bible. Therefore, we must turn our attention to Paul's letters if we are to do justice to the biblical teaching on predestination. In fact, Paul has so much to say about election that we will need two chapters to treat it adequately. The chapter after this one will focus on the three most important Pauline texts on election: Ephesians 1:4–5, 11; Romans 8:29–30; and Romans 9:6–24. In this chapter we will consider other passages where Paul mentions the concept of predestination. We will first treat the election of Israel and then focus on the topic that Paul himself focuses on—the election of Christians.

1. William W. Klein, *The New Chosen People: A Corporate View of Election* (Grand Rapids: Academie Books, 1990), 158.

- The Election of Israel
  - Romans 11:1–7
  - Romans 11:25–28

- The Election of Christians
  - Romans 8:33
  - Romans 16:13
  - Colossians 3:12
  - 1 Thessalonians 1:4–5
  - 1 Thessalonians 5:9
  - 2 Thessalonians 2:13
  - 2 Timothy 1:9
  - 2 Timothy 2:10
  - Titus 1:1

The Election of Israel

As we have seen, the major focus of the Old Testament concerning election is that God chose Israel alone out of all the nations. Not so the New Testament. Here the chief focus is on the election of the church, the New Testament people of God. Nevertheless, although the matter is debatable, I am of the opinion that Paul in Romans 11 reaffirms the Old Testament teaching concerning the election of ethnic Israel.

Romans 11:1–7

I ask, then, has God rejected his people? By no means! For I myself am an Israelite, a descendant of Abraham, a member of the tribe of Benjamin. God has not rejected his people whom he foreknew. Do you not know what the Scripture says of Elijah, how he appeals to God against Israel? "Lord, they have killed your prophets, they have demolished your altars, and I alone am left, and they seek my life." But what is God's reply to him? "I have kept for myself seven thousand men who have not bowed the knee to Baal." So too at the present time there is a remnant, chosen by grace. But if it is by grace, it is no longer on the basis of works; otherwise grace would no longer be grace.

What then? Israel failed to obtain what it was seeking. The elect obtained it, but the rest were hardened.

Paul has just taught that the majority of Israelites in the first century have rejected Christ: "But of Israel he says, 'All day long I have held out my hands to a disobedient and contrary people'" (Rom. 10:21, quoting Isa. 65:2). This prompts him to ask the question that begins Romans 11: has God totally rejected his people Israel? Paul answers in the negative, naming himself as an example of an Israelite whom God has saved.

The apostle then cites the Old Testament account of Elijah who, after his mighty victory over the prophets of Baal on Mount Carmel, fled from the wrath of the evil queen, Jezebel. Elijah is despondent: "Lord, they have killed your prophets, they have demolished your altars, and I alone am left, and they seek my life" (Rom. 11:3, quoting 1 Kings 19:10, 14).

The Lord mercifully assures the depressed prophet: "I have kept for myself seven thousand men who have not bowed the knee to Baal" (Rom. 11:4, quoting 1 Kings 19:18). Although the dejected Elijah thought that he was the only faithful Israelite, in reality God had preserved for himself seven thousand not guilty of spiritual adultery with Baal.

Paul comes to the climax: "So too at the present time there is a remnant, chosen by grace. But if it is by grace, it is no longer on the basis of works; otherwise grace would no longer be grace" (Rom. 11:5). As in Elijah's time, so, too, in the first century there was a believing remnant of Israel, chosen by God's grace. This is how Paul accounts for the fact that, unlike the majority of Israelites, he and many others have trusted Christ as Lord—it is due to the electing grace of God.

The apostle then makes a very difficult statement: "What then? Israel failed to obtain what it was seeking. The elect obtained it, but the rest were hardened" (Rom. 11:7). Here Paul divides first-century Israelites into "the elect" and "the rest." As a whole the chosen nation rejected its Messiah and did not obtain salvation, but because of God's differentiating grace many believed and were saved. What about those who did not believe? They were hardened. Paul then quotes Old Testament passages that speak of God's hardening of Israel: Deuteronomy 29:4, Isaiah 29:10, and Psalm 69:22–23.

If any Israelites in Paul's day trusted Christ, it was due to God's electing grace. Because Paul distinguishes "the rest" from "the elect," it follows that God did not choose all Israelites to be saved. But Paul's focus is not on the justice of God's not choosing some; it is on the miracle of God's choosing many. And we will leave this difficult matter there until we discuss double predestination in the conclusion of this book.

Romans 11:25-28

> Lest you be wise in your own conceits, I want you to understand this mystery, brothers: a partial hardening has come upon Israel, until the fullness of the Gentiles has come in. And in this way all Israel will be saved, as it is written, "The Deliverer will come from Zion, he will banish ungodliness from Jacob"; "and this will be my covenant with them when I take away their sins." As regards the gospel, they are enemies of God for your sake. But as regards election, they are beloved for the sake of their forefathers.

Paul teaches Hebrew Christians and Gentile Christians in Rome concerning God's dealings with Jews and Gentiles in the new covenant. Israel, the Old Testament people of God, in rejecting its Messiah has experienced a hardening in regard to spiritual things. Israel in general is unresponsive to the gospel of Christ. But Paul labels this hardening "partial." It will last until the full number of the Gentiles to be saved have come into the new covenant. "And in this way all Israel will be saved" (Rom. 11:26). This much-debated verse has been variously interpreted, as Anthony Hoekema helpfully discusses.[2] Some scholars have taken it to mean spiritual Israel, the church.[3] The New Testament frequently refers to the church as spiritual Israel, but as Hoekema notes:

> In Romans 9–11 the term *Israel* occurs eleven times; in each of the ten instances other than 11:26 where the term is used, it points unmistakably to the Jews in distinction from the Gentiles. What reason is there for accepting a different meaning of the term here? Why should Paul suddenly shift from the natural meaning of the term *Israel* to a wider figurative meaning? Is not the very point of Romans 11:25–26a to say something about both Jews and Gentiles?[4]

I find Hoekema's reasoning convincing, and many others reach the same conclusion.[5] This means that "all Israel" in Romans 11:26 refers not to spiritual Israel, the church, but to ethnic Israel, the physical descendants of Abraham. This view has three subsets. "All Israel," understood as ethnic Jews, has been taken to mean (1) the sum total of Jews who trust Christ between his two advents, (2) a large harvest of Jews at the return of Christ, and (3) a geopolitical entity in Palestine (the dispensational view). I favor a combination of the first two subsets: "And in this way all Israel will be saved" means that God will bring to himself in salvation the sum total of Israelites who believe in Christ between the first and second comings, with an emphasis on a large conversion near the time of Christ's second coming.

2. Anthony A. Hoekema, *The Bible and the Future* (Grand Rapids: Eerdmans, 1979), 139–47.

3. For instance, see O. Palmer Robertson, *The Israel of God* (Phillipsburg, NJ: P&R Publishing, 2000).

4. Hoekema, *The Bible and the Future*, 144.

5. Among them are John Murray, *The Epistle to the Romans*, New International Commentary on the New Testament (Grand Rapids: Eerdmans, 1968), 96–98; C. E. B. Cranfield, *A Critical and Exegetical Commentary on the Epistle to the Romans*, 2 vols., International Critical Commentary (Edinburgh: T&T Clark, 2001–2004), 576–77; C. K. Barrett, *The Epistle to the Romans*, 2nd ed. (London: Hendrickson, 1991), 223–24; Douglas J. Moo, *The Epistle to the Romans*, New International Commentary on the New Testament (Grand Rapids: Eerdmans, 1996), 720–23; and Thomas R. Schreiner, *Romans* (Grand Rapids: Baker, 1998), 615–19.

This conclusion is reinforced by Paul's words in Romans 11:28: "As regards the gospel, they are enemies of God for your sake. But as regards election, they are beloved for the sake of their forefathers." It is important to keep the pronouns straight in this verse. Paul is addressing the Gentile Christians in the Roman congregation. He means, therefore, that as respects the gospel, the Jews are enemies of God; but that as respects God's election, they are loved by God because of the patriarchs.

Israel of the first century (or the twenty-first century, for that matter) is an anomaly! As concerns the gospel of Christ, which so many Gentiles have believed that the Jews are a minority among God's New Testament people, Israel is an enemy of God. But—amazingly—as concerns God's choice of Israel in the Old Testament, Israel is still loved by God for the sake of Abraham, Isaac, and Jacob. Israel at one and the same time is hated and loved by God!

Paul's immediately following words are important: "For the gifts and the calling of God are irrevocable" (Rom. 11:29). God's choice of Israel in the Old Testament is permanent; he will not go back on his promises to the Jews. This statement, however, needs a couple of qualifications. First, as Romans so eloquently declares: "The gospel . . . is the power of God for salvation to everyone who believes, to the Jew first and also to the Greek" (Rom. 1:16). Since the coming of Christ, no one, including Jews, will ever be saved apart from faith in him.

Second, if I have correctly interpreted Romans 11:26–29, it declares that God is not finished with ethnic Israel, with the physical descendants of Abraham. But it says nothing about the nation of Israel. While it speaks of ethnic Israel, it does not deal with national Israel. The New Testament seems to be silent concerning the modern state of Israel.

God, long ago, chose the nation of Israel out of all the nations to be his people. Romans reveals that even though most Jews today reject the gospel of God's Son, God still holds out his hands to his disobedient people, inviting them to trust their Messiah Jesus as Lord and Savior. All who do so become a part of the one

Christian church, which is composed of believing Jews and Gentiles. But all Jews who reject Jesus, although they are objects of God's affection as descendants of the patriarchs, are his enemies because they reject the gospel. Although they belong to the ethnic group that God chose with a historical election, if they persist in unbelief they reveal that they have not been chosen with an eternal election.

The Election of Christians

Reformed scholars do not unanimously agree with my conclusions in the previous section, where I maintain that God's choice of ethnic Jews in the Old Testament is reaffirmed in Romans 11. But we are united in affirming that the apple of Paul's eye concerning election is the individuals who make up the Christian church.

Romans 8:33

Paul appeals to election as one part of a sustained argument for God's preservation of his people in Romans 8:28–39. The apostle writes: "Who shall bring any charge against God's elect? It is God who justifies" (v. 33). Here, as often in verses 31–35, Paul uses a rhetorical question. His question does not expect an answer; instead, he uses an interrogative form to press home a truth: no one can successfully press charges against God's chosen people! The language is legal. The phrase "bring charges" is used by the town clerk who acts to quiet an angry mob of his fellow Ephesians, enraged by Christian preaching against their goddess Artemis and her idols: "If therefore Demetrius and the craftsmen with him have a complaint against anyone, the courts are open, and there are proconsuls. Let them *bring charges* against one another" (Acts 19:38).

"Who shall bring any charge against God's elect?" Although Paul is not seeking an answer, several come to mind: Satan, demons, and human enemies of the faith all would like to condemn God's people before God. Paul's point is that neither these foes nor any others will be able to condemn God's people. Why? Paul's next words provide the answer: "It is God who justifies." The case against God's chosen ones has already gone to the supreme court of the universe, and God the Judge, who knows their sins better than they themselves do, has pronounced them "righteous." No one will ever overturn that verdict.

Paul could have used many terms to describe Christians when he asked rhetorically: "Who shall bring any charge against [them]?" He could have called them "believers," "saints," "beloved," or "brothers." But he did not; instead, he called them "God's elect." Why? To designate them as people whom God had chosen for salvation. Their election was so important that the apostle could refer to them simply as "God's chosen ones" or "God's elect ones." Perhaps his thought harks back to Romans 8:30: "And those whom he predestined . . . he also justified . . ." The people whom God predestined for salvation will not fail to be justified, and their justification by God himself means that no charges of condemnation will ever be successfully brought against them.

Romans 16:13

Near the end of his epistle to the Romans, Paul conveys extensive greetings to the church. He greets twenty-six persons by name in this section and uses a variety of expressions to describe them, including "fellow workers" (Rom. 16:3, 9), "beloved" (vv. 5, 8, 12), "fellow prisoners" (v. 7), "approved" (v. 10), and "workers" (v. 12). One of his greetings reads, "Greet Rufus, chosen in the Lord; also his mother, who has been a mother to me as well" (v. 13). Paul did not consider predestination a strange or harmful teaching that was to be avoided. Indeed, it was as natural for him to refer to fellow believers as "chosen in the Lord" as it was for him to refer to them as "beloved" or "approved." Paul regards individual Christians, such as Rufus, as chosen by God for salvation. This fact need not be hidden, but could be expressed in a warm greeting to fellow Christians.

Colossians 3:12

After teaching that believers have been united to Christ in his death (Col. 2:20; 3:3) and resurrection (3:1, 3), Paul applies that teaching in practical ways. The Colossians (as crucified with Christ) are to "put to death" sinful attitudes and practices (3:5–11) and (as risen with Christ) to "put on" godly ones (vv. 12–17). As he shifts from putting to death to putting on, the apostle instructs his readers: "Put on then, as *God's chosen ones*, holy and beloved, compassion, kindness, humility, meekness, and patience, bearing with one another and, if one has a complaint against another, forgiving each other; as the Lord has forgiven you, so you also must forgive" (vv. 12–13).

Paul addresses the Colossian Christians as "God's chosen ones, holy and beloved." This threefold address describes them as predestined by God for salvation, as his saints, and as dearly loved by him. Paul reminds the Colossians of their identity in order to motivate them to live for God. All three descriptions are important. The believers need to be reminded of God the Father's love. They need to remember that they are saints who should live accordingly. Furthermore, in order that they might be strengthened to honor their Father, Paul wants them to remember that he chose them to belong to him. Once more we notice that it is as natural for Paul to refer to believers as "chosen" as it is for him to call them "holy and beloved."

1 Thessalonians 1:4–5

After his salutation and giving thanks to God for the Thessalonian church, Paul writes: "For we know, brothers loved by God, that he has chosen you, because our gospel came to you not only in word, but also in power and in the Holy Spirit and with full conviction" (1 Thess. 1:4–5). Paul, addressing the believers in Thessalonica as brothers and sisters in Christ "loved by God," expresses confidence that God has chosen them for salvation. How does Paul know God's election? Has he been able to probe the mind of God before the creation of the world to learn his plans?

On the contrary, Paul says that he knows the Thessalonians are elect "because our gospel came to you not only in word, but also in power and in the Holy Spirit and with full conviction" (v. 5). God's eternal predestination of his people is known only when they believe the gospel of his Son.

Here Paul connects predestination with calling, as he does elsewhere in his writings (e.g., Rom. 8:30; 9:22–24). We do not have direct access to the mind of God concerning election. But we do know what his Word reveals: that God has chosen people for eternal life, and we learn that he has chosen them when he effectively summons them to himself in the preaching of the gospel. God who has chosen is the one who causes the gospel to come with power, the Spirit, and conviction, as he did in Thessalonica.

1 Thessalonians 5:9

Paul, instructing the Thessalonian believers concerning the second coming of Christ, reminds them that "the day of the Lord will come like a thief in the night" upon unbelievers (1 Thess. 5:2). He means that Christ's return will be unexpected by the unsaved; indeed, they will be jolted out of a false sense of security and "will not escape" (v. 3). But Paul's readers are Christians, who need not fear the return of Christ. They do not belong to the darkness but the light. Thus, they must be vigilant, and hold fast to faith, hope, and love; but they have nothing to fear.

Why is the apostle confident concerning the fate of the Thessalonians? He writes: "For God has not *destined* us for wrath, but to obtain salvation through our Lord Jesus Christ, who died for us so that whether we are awake or asleep we might live with him" (vv. 9–10). The standard lexicon of New Testament Greek gives "destine or appoint someone to or for something" as the meaning of the word translated "destined" in this passage.[6] A similar use of the same word is found in 1 Timothy 1:12: "I thank him

---

6. William F. Arndt and F. Wilbur Gingrich, *A Greek–English Lexicon of the New Testament and Other Early Christian Literature*, ed. F. Wilbur Gingrich and Fredrick W. Danker, revised and augmented from Walter Bauer's 5th ed. (Chicago: University of Chicago Press, 1979), 816.

who has given me strength, Christ Jesus our Lord, because he judged me faithful, *appointing* me to his service, though formerly I was a blasphemer, persecutor, and insolent opponent" (1 Tim. 1:12–13).

Contrary to certain claims, Paul here teaches that God destines some people for salvation (and not just for service). Indeed, the fact that God ordained the Thessalonians for salvation gives the apostle confidence that they will be saved. Notice that while Paul does not teach that the Thessalonians' predestination is based on their faithfulness or holiness, he regards his teaching of predestination as compatible with exhortations to faithfulness and holiness in 1 Thessalonians 5:8, 10.

2 Thessalonians 2:13

In contrast with the wicked, who spurn the claims of the gospel and are unsaved (2 Thess. 2:10, 12), the Thessalonians believed in the truth and were saved (v. 13). Paul directs thanksgiving to God for their salvation: "But we ought always to thank God for you, brothers loved by the Lord, because from the beginning God chose you to be saved" (v. 13 NIV). Although some manuscripts and translations (e.g., the ESV) read: "God chose you *as the first-fruits* to be saved," the more intelligible reading is "God chose you *from the beginning* to be saved."[7]

God loved and chose the Thessalonians for salvation, and also planned the means by which they would taste that salvation: initial sanctification and faith. "From the beginning God chose you to be saved through the sanctifying work of the Spirit and through belief in the truth" (v. 13 NIV). God chose to save the Thessalonians, bringing his grace to bear on their lives when the

---

7. Charles A. Wanamaker argues that "the textual evidence is not sufficient in itself to make a decision between the two possibilities." He says that although "Paul nowhere else uses ἀπ᾽ ἀρχῆς to denote 'from the beginning of time,'" that expression "makes good sense in the context, whereas it is difficult to find a satisfactory meaning for ἀπαρχήν." *Epistle to the Thessalonians: A Commentary on the Greek Text*, New International Greek Testament Commentary (Grand Rapids: Eerdmans, 1990), 266. For another view, see F. F. Bruce, *1 & 2 Thessalonians*, Word Biblical Commentary (Waco, TX: Word, 1982), 190.

Holy Spirit set them apart for salvation so that they believed the gospel. Paul ranges far and wide in matters pertaining to salvation when he writes: "To this he called you through our gospel, so that you may obtain the glory of our Lord Jesus Christ" (v. 14). The apostle links God's choosing the Thessalonians "from the beginning," his calling them to salvation in Christ, and their future glorification. Salvation is God's work from beginning to end: he chooses, he calls, and he glorifies.

Paul here affirms that there is an election that results in salvation. It includes the individuals who corporately constitute the church in Thessalonica. God brings his plans to pass and sends his Spirit to work in their lives, that they might believe the truth and be saved. Paul teaches by example that it is fitting to give thanks to God for his grace shown in predestinating and saving his people. It is also fitting for Paul to follow his statements of God's sovereign grace with practical exhortations to steadfastness (v. 15). Although God's choices are not based on foreseen faithfulness, his choices are compatible with exhortations to faithfulness.

2 Timothy 1:9

After greetings and expressions of encouragement, Paul urges Timothy to be willing to suffer for Christ. Timothy is not to rely on his own strength, however, but is to suffer "by the power of God, who saved us . . . , not because of our works but because of his own purpose and grace" (2 Tim. 1:8–9). No sooner does Paul speak of God's power than he mentions salvation. God's power and our salvation go together in the apostle's mind.

Our salvation, Paul insists, is "not because of our works," that is, not based on anything that we could do. To the contrary, we are saved entirely because of God's "own purpose and grace" (v. 9). Here is a summary of the Bible's teaching on the ultimate cause of the salvation of all who are saved—it is because of God's purpose and grace. Both concepts deserve unpacking. We are saved by God's purpose, his resolve, his plan to save sinners.

God exerted his will and chose us to be saved. We are saved by his grace, his kindness, his compassion, bestowed in spite of our demerits. God's will to choose sinners for salvation cannot be separated from his love. To summarize: we are delivered because of God's compassionate will, his sovereign mercy.

Paul specifies that this saving grace was given to "us in Christ Jesus before the ages began, and . . . now has been manifested through the appearing of our Savior Christ Jesus" (vv. 9–10). The apostle distinguishes between God's eternal planning of salvation and its appearing in the life and ministry of Jesus. At least two things are noteworthy here.

First, God granted grace to his people "before the ages began"—or, more literally, "before eternal ages." This is one of three times that Scripture says that God planned our salvation before creation. Ephesians 1:4 declares that God "chose us in him [Christ] before the foundation of the world" for salvation. Revelation 17:8 teaches that those "whose names have not been written in the book of life from the foundation of the world will marvel to see the beast," that is, will be misled. These three passages locate salvation "before" or "from" the creation of anything, including human beings. They imply that God took nothing into account except his own "purpose and grace" when he chose to save us. Notice how Paul combines a denial that our deeds had anything to do with salvation with his crediting our salvation to God's granting us grace before creation: "God . . . saved us . . . , not because of our works but because of his own . . . grace, which he gave us in Christ Jesus before the ages began" (1 Tim. 1:8–9). William Klein's summary deserves attention: "We find affirmation that Christians can attribute their saved status solely to God's purpose and grace."[8]

Second, before creation God granted us his grace "in Christ Jesus" (2 Tim. 1:9). This is an echo of Ephesians 1:4, where the Father's choosing of sinners for final sanctification was a choosing "in him [namely, Christ] before the foundation of the

8. Klein, *The New Chosen People*, 171.

world." In the discussion of Ephesians 1:4 in the next chapter, I will treat the Arminian view that being chosen in Christ means that God chose people based on his foreknowledge of their faith. At present, note that 2 Timothy 1:9 contains no mention of human beings' response to the gospel. Rather, the focus is on God, who gave grace to his people before creation and did so "in Christ Jesus." Paul means that God's gracious election included his resolve to join to Christ the people whom he had chosen. God not only elected a people for salvation, but also planned to unite them to his Son, that they might actually experience this salvation. Union with Christ was not an afterthought of God. Instead, when God predestined sinners to salvation, he also planned to join them to the Son (by sending his Son to die and rise again for them and by sending the Spirit). The addition of the words "in Christ Jesus" thus underscores the grace of God, who "before the ages began" purposed to unite the elect to Christ.

Paul's extolling of God's purpose and grace was designed to embolden Timothy—and us—to serve the Lord. The apostle's words about God's planning salvation before creation and manifesting it in the person and work of Christ encourage Timothy to live for him without fear, even if it means suffering. May his words do the same for us.

2 Timothy 2:10

Paul exhorts Timothy to be strong in the Lord, to teach others, and to suffer for Christ (2 Tim. 2:1–7). Then the apostle reminds him of the content and power of the gospel: "Remember Jesus Christ, risen from the dead, the offspring of David, as preached in my gospel, for which I am suffering, bound with chains as a criminal. But the word of God is not bound!" (vv. 8–9). Christ, as preached by Paul, is both God (as his resurrection attests) and human (as his lineage attests). Paul is in chains, but the gospel will never be bound because God mightily uses his Word in spite of human opposition.

Because God's Word cannot be imprisoned, Paul endures much suffering in order to promote the message of salvation: "Therefore I endure everything for the sake of the elect, that they also may obtain the salvation that is in Christ Jesus with eternal glory" (2 Tim. 2:10). Paul could have said that he endures everything for the sake of believers, the saints, the people of God, or the church. Instead, he says that he endures everything "for the sake of the elect." Paul does not shy away from designating the people of God as elect, or chosen ones.

The apostle has a specific purpose in mind for his suffering: he endures much for those who are chosen so "that they also may obtain ... salvation" (v. 10). As we saw in the last passage, God chose persons for salvation "before the ages began" (2 Tim. 1:9). But they are not saved then; they are saved during their lifetimes when they believe in Christ. Of course, salvation is "in Christ Jesus" because he alone is the way to the Father (John 14:6) and salvation is found in his name alone (Acts 4:12). And as a result of God's grace, salvation brings "eternal glory" to all who turn from their sins and trust the Son of God, who loved them and gave himself for them.

Paul and Timothy may suffer, even with imprisonment. But nothing can stop the risen Christ, the invincible Word, and the Father from bringing to God those whom he has chosen. Armed with such expectancy, Timothy is to fight the good fight of faith, confident that he is on the winning side—that of God Almighty.

Titus 1:1

Paul's salutation in his letter to Titus, stripped down to essentials, reads: "Paul, a servant of God and an apostle of Jesus Christ . . . ; to Titus, my true child in a common faith: Grace and peace from God the Father and Christ Jesus our Savior" (Titus 1:1, 4). Paul, however, does not present a bare salutation but, as is his custom, dresses it up in fancy garb:

> Paul, a servant of God and an apostle of Jesus Christ, for the sake of the faith of God's elect and their knowledge of the truth,

which accords with godliness, in hope of eternal life, which
God, who never lies, promised before the ages began and at
the proper time manifested in his word through the preaching
with which I have been entrusted by the command of God our
Savior. (Titus 1:1–3)

The apostle writes to Titus for the sake of God's people and their
knowledge of the gospel, which promotes godliness. He writes
with a hope of final salvation, promised by the truthful God before
eternal ages and now revealed through the apostles' preaching.
Paul designates God's people "the elect of God" or "God's chosen
ones," and in so doing introduces another reference to election in
his letters. He does not go into detail here concerning predestination but simply says that he writes "for" or "for the sake of" the
faith and knowledge of the truth of God's chosen ones.[9]

As he was in 2 Timothy 2:10, so here Paul is concerned that
the people whom God has chosen will come to believe the gospel
and be saved. God chooses people before creation, but they are
not actually saved from their sins until they come to know the
Lord. In 2 Timothy 2:10, Paul's desire for the elect to be saved
led him to endure suffering. Here the apostle writes the letter to
Titus, at least in part, so that the elect will come to saving faith
in Christ. Plainly, Paul did not regard the doctrine of election as
a hindrance to vital service to God and evangelism. Rather, he
suffered, wrote epistles, and served God with a confidence that
the One who chose sinners for himself before creation would
bring them to a saving knowledge of his Son in time and space
through the ministries of his servants, including Paul himself.

Conclusion

This chapter has explored a minor theme, God's election of
Israel, and a major one, his election of the church.

9. Arndt and Gingrich, *A Greek–English Lexicon of the New Testament*, 406–7: κατά
(*kata*), "for the purpose of, for, to . . . Tit 1:1."

God's Election of Israel

God's choice of Israel to be his people is a significant theme in the Old Testament but is mentioned in the New Testament only in Romans 11. When Paul divides first-century Israel into "the elect" who obtained salvation and "the rest" who did not (Rom. 11:7), he indicates that all Jews are historically elect, but only some are eternally elect.

Although the matter is debated, I understand Paul's words "And in this way all Israel will be saved" (Rom. 11:26) to indicate that many physical descendants of Abraham will come to Christ in the time between his first and second comings and that there will be a large spiritual harvest of Jews near the second coming.

Ever since Israel rejected its Messiah, Jesus, in the first century, Jews have stood in an unusual relation to God, according to Romans 11:28: "As regards the gospel, they are enemies of God for your sake. But as regards election, they are beloved for the sake of their forefathers." Jews put themselves against God when they reject the gospel, but they are still objects of God's affection because of his promises to Abraham, Isaac, and Jacob.

God's Election of the Church

Among Paul's designations for God's people are "chosen ones," "the elect," and "God's elect." The apostle uses these descriptions to refer to individuals ("Rufus, chosen in the Lord," Rom. 16:13) and groups of Christians (Rom. 8:33; Col. 3:12; 2 Tim. 2:10; Titus 1:1). Paul thus does not regard calling people "the elect" as strange, harmful, or something to be hidden. Rather, "chosen ones" comes easily to his mind and lips.

Paul teaches that God granted people grace before creation: "God . . . saved us . . . , not because of our works but because of his own purpose and grace, which he gave us in Christ Jesus before the ages began" (2 Tim. 1:8–9). That is, before we even existed, let alone did anything good or bad, God placed his love upon us. The same passage teaches that election is based on God's purpose and grace, not on anything that human beings do. This

101

teaching does not fit with the Arminian idea that God chooses based on his foreknowledge of faith in his Son.

Election is "in Christ Jesus" (2 Tim. 1:9); that is, God not only chose a people as his own but also planned to join them to Christ so that they might experience salvation. In fact, God's predestination of persons is for the very purpose of saving them: "God has not destined us for wrath, but to obtain salvation through our Lord Jesus Christ" (1 Thess. 5:9; see also 2 Thess. 2:13). This, too, contradicts Arminian teaching when it claims that election is for service, not salvation; in reality it is for both purposes.

We know that people are chosen, Paul teaches, not by prying into God's eternal counsels, but by seeing them come to Christ: "For we know, brothers loved by God, that he has chosen you, because our gospel came to you not only in word, but also in power and in the Holy Spirit and with full conviction" (1 Thess. 1:4–5).

The apostle holds that God's eternal election of a people has great practical import. God's people are safe in Christ because God has declared them righteous and no one can overturn his verdict (Rom. 8:33). Predestination brings strong motivation for giving God thanks (2 Thess. 2:13), and it emboldens us to suffer for the gospel (2 Tim. 1:8–9), that the elect might be saved (2 Tim. 2:10). Paul pens his epistle to Titus, at least in part, "for the sake of the faith of God's elect" (Titus 1:1).

Although we have surveyed eleven election passages from Paul's letters in this chapter, we have not even looked at the three most important ones. It is to these passages that we now turn.

Election in Paul's Epistles, Part 2

Although the idea of election occurs frequently in Paul's letters, in three places he gives it extended treatment:

- Ephesians 1:4–5, 11
- Romans 8:29–30
- Romans 9:6–24

We will investigate these passages in turn.

Ephesians 1:4–5, 11

Ephesians 1:3–14, one long sentence in Greek, divides topically into three sections, each marked by the refrain "to the praise of his glorious grace" (v. 6) and its echoes in verses 12 and 14 (Eph. 1:3–6, 7–12, 13–14). Each section is characterized by the work of one person of the Trinity. The Father chooses people for salvation (vv. 3–6), the Son redeems them (vv. 7–12), and the Spirit is the "guarantee" of their "inheritance" (vv. 13–14). And all of this is for "the praise of his glory" (vv. 12, 14).

The theological context, then, for Paul's teaching of predestination in Ephesians 1 is praise directed to the Trinity for such a great salvation. Within that context Paul expands our knowledge by giving at least four truths about God's election: its timing, its basis, its results, and its being "in Christ."

The Timing of Election

For the first time in the Bible we are told the timing of election: God the Father "chose us in him [Christ] before the foundation of the world" (Eph. 1:4). Before creating anything, the Father chose people to belong to him. Why does Paul speak concerning the timing of predestination? For the same reason that he introduces a time element in Romans 9:11–12: *"Though they were not yet born and had done nothing either good or bad—in order that God's purpose of election might continue, not because of works but because of his call—she [Rebecca] was told, 'The older will serve the younger.'"* Paul says that God chose Jacob over Esau before either one was born in order to accentuate the fact that election is based on the free will of God, not that of human beings. God's choice of the twins before birth shows that God did not base his choice on anything they did but on his own sovereign purpose.

Similarly, when Paul says that God chose us before the creation of the world, he emphasizes God's purpose in election. We obviously did not even exist before the creation of the world and could not, therefore, contribute anything to our predestination. Paul teaches the same truth in 2 Timothy 1:9, where he describes God's grace as that which "he gave us in Christ Jesus before the ages began."

We conclude, then, that Paul's locating election before creation flies in the face of the Arminian concept of conditional election: the idea that God chose us based on his foreseeing our faith in his Son. To the contrary, God chose us before we *were* in order that, after he had called us to himself in salvation, we would praise him for his free grace.

The Basis of Election

Sometimes it is said that Ephesians 1 talks about the results of election, but not its basis. In fact, it teaches both. More plainly than anyone else in Scripture, Paul affirms that God elected his people for salvation out of his love and sovereign will. God's love is the basis of predestination. *"In love* he predestined us for adoption through Jesus Christ . . . , to the praise of *his glorious grace"* (Eph. 1:4b–5).

God's sovereignty is also the basis of election, as we learn from the same verses: "In love he predestined us for adoption through Jesus Christ, *according to the purpose of his will."* The Father's election of people for salvation is made according to his divine purpose and free will. And verse 11 reiterates: "In him we have obtained an inheritance, having been predestined according to the purpose of him who works all things according to the counsel of his will." How could it be said more emphatically that predestination is based on God's sovereign purpose? Paul explains that God makes all things conform to his will, including his free choice of human beings to be his own.

The gospel of John and the book of Acts teach that the basis for election resides in God, not in foreseen human response. But no more details are given. Paul fleshes out the doctrine by teaching that predestination is based on both God's love and his sovereignty. It is helpful to combine the two aspects—ultimately God's election of us depends on his free grace, sovereign mercy, gracious will, and loving choice. Paul's teaching on the basis of election in Ephesians 1 cuts across the grain of Arminian theology. Election is based on God's grace and will, not foreseen faith as Arminianism maintains (vv. 3–4, 11).

The Results of Election

Paul also teaches that election produces results. The Father "chose us . . . , that we should be holy and blameless before him" (Eph. 1:4). This means that election results in sanctification. "In love he predestined us for adoption" (vv. 4b–5). This means that predestination results in adoption. Sanctification and adoption are two ways of speaking about salvation. God sets his own apart unto holiness (sanctification); he gives them the status of children in his family (adoption). It is clear, then, that election results in salvation (sanctification and adoption). As a result, Arminianism errs when it claims that predestination pertains to service and not salvation. It pertains to both.

Election "in Christ"

One important matter remains in our study of election in Ephesians 1. What is the meaning of election or predestination "in him [Christ]" (Eph. 1:4, 11)? Union with Christ is God's gracious act of spiritually joining to his Son those who were previously "separated from Christ . . . , having no hope and without God in the world" (Eph. 2:12). Paul frequently (not always) employs "in Christ" and "in him" to refer to union with Christ. He does this eight times in Ephesians 1 (vv. 1, 3, 4, 6, 7, 9, 11, 13), two of which speak of God's choosing us "in him" (vv. 4, 11). How does Paul's regular use of "in Christ" differ from his use of "in Christ" to refer to election? The difference is temporal. When speaking of predestination, Paul teaches that God chose people in Christ *before the foundation of the world* (v. 4). But in every other case when Paul uses the phrase "in Christ" (except for 2 Timothy 1:9), he tells of God's uniting people to Christ *in history*.

God's choice of us "in him before the foundation of the world" (v. 4; see also v. 11) speaks of our union with Christ before creation. But these words cannot speak of actual union with Christ, for before our creation by God, we did not exist. Instead, Paul speaks of God's plan to unite us to Christ. Therefore, the meaning of the words "he chose us in him before the foundation of the world" is that God not only chose to save his people, but also planned the means by which they would experience that salvation; he purposed to unite them spiritually to his Son.

Arminian Approaches

What is the Arminian view of election "in Christ"? Jack Cottrell explains:

106

God foreknows whether an individual will meet the *conditions* for salvation which he has sovereignly imposed. . . . The basic and all-encompassing condition is whether a person is *in Christ*, namely whether one has entered into a saving union with Christ by means of which he shares in all the benefits of Christ's redeeming work. . . . This is the import of Eph. 1:4, which says that "He chose us in Him"—in Christ.[1]

Arminianism holds that election "in Christ" means that God chose individuals for salvation based on his foreknowledge of who would be "in Christ" by believing in him. Is this view correct? When Paul writes, "He chose us in him before the foundation of the world," he does not mention a condition that sinners must meet in order for God to choose them. In fact, Paul's words do not speak of the response of human beings at all, but of the sovereign plan of God. Arminians read foreseen faith into the words in an attempt to harmonize their view of conditional election with the apostle's words. But the attempt fails.

There are at least two other Arminian approaches to this passage. First, William Klein is representative of some who maintain that "the focus is not on the selection of individuals, but the group of those chosen."[2] It is true that the pronouns that Paul uses in Ephesians 1 to describe the persons chosen by God are plural and not singular. He does not say that God "chose me," but that God "chose us." But this does not prove that predestination to salvation here is corporate and not individual. Paul does not address the epistle to the Ephesians to an individual, as he does the pastoral epistles, but to a church or churches made up of believers. So we would expect Paul to use plural pronouns. With regard to election being individual or corporate, it is not a matter of "either/or" but of "both/and." God chooses individuals for salvation (sanctification and adoption; vv. 3–4), individuals who make up the church. God chose Jews ("we who were the

---

1. Jack Cottrell, "Conditional Election," in *Grace Unlimited*, ed. Clark H. Pinnock (Minneapolis: Bethany House, 1975), 61 (italics in original).
2. William W. Klein, *The New Chosen People: A Corporate View of Election* (Grand Rapids: Academie Books, 1990), 179.

first to hope in Christ," v. 12) and Gentiles ("you also," v. 13) to constitute the church.

Second, Arminians have sometimes interpreted Paul's statement that God "chose us in him before the foundation of the world" to mean that primarily God chose Christ and only secondarily chose people for salvation, specifically foreseen believers. Jerry Walls and Joseph Dongell explain:

> Jesus Christ himself is the chosen one, the predestined one. Whenever one is incorporated into him by grace through faith, one comes to share in Jesus' special status as chosen by God. . . . This view of election most fully accounts for the corporate nature of salvation, the decisive role of faith and the overarching reliability of God's bringing his people to their destined end.[3]

God did choose Christ to be the divine-human Redeemer, but that doctrine is not taught in Ephesians 1. Rather, Paul teaches that God "chose *us* in him" (Eph. 1:4). The Father chose people with the view of uniting them to his Son. Although Karl Barth, no Arminian, argued at length that Ephesians 1:4 teaches that Christ was elect, it simply is not taught there.[4]

Furthermore, when Walls and Dongell say, "Whenever one is incorporated into him by grace through faith, one comes to share in Jesus' special status as chosen by God," they read conditional election into Paul's words. Ephesians 1:4 does not even mention the response of human beings to the gospel.

Romans 8:29–30

After urging the Romans to view present struggles in the light of future glory (Rom. 8:18–27), Paul writes, "And we know that for those who love God all things work together for good, for those

---

3. Jerry L. Walls and Joseph R. Dongell, *Why I Am Not a Calvinist* (Downers Grove, IL: InterVarsity Press, 2004), 76.

4. For Barth's views, see pages 33–34 of this book.

who are called according to his purpose" (v. 28). In context, Paul means that even while suffering, Christians can be confident that God is working for their ultimate good. He explains why: "For those whom he foreknew he also predestined to be conformed to the image of his Son, in order that he might be the firstborn among many brothers. And those whom he predestined he also called, and those whom he called he also justified, and those whom he justified he also glorified" (vv. 29–30). We can be sure that God will do all for our ultimate good because he has already brought about our greatest good—he purposed and accomplished our salvation from beginning to end.

Paul employs five simple past-tense (aorist) verbs to depict God's deeds. God foreknew, predestined, called, justified, and glorified "those who love" him (Rom. 8:28). These verbs all have the same subject—God—and the same object—Christians. Here is a summary of the meaning of the five verbs, starting with the last: God glorifies his own when he brings them to see Christ's glory and be changed by it. He justifies them by crediting Christ's righteousness to them and declaring them righteous. He calls them by causing the gospel to reach their ears and to take root in their hearts. He predestines them by selecting them before-hand for salvation. Finally, he foreknows his people. But what does that mean? Because foreknowledge is so controversial, it deserves special attention.

Foreknowledge

Arminians and Calvinists differ in their understanding of foreknowledge. Arminians teach that God foreknows or foresees what people will do with the gospel and bases election on his foresight. This is known as conditional election because God's choosing of people for salvation is conditioned on his foreseeing their belief or unbelief. Calvinists beg to differ and usually hold that God's foreknowledge in Romans 8:29 and related passages means his choosing of people for salvation. Although it is possible for "foreknow" to mean "choose" (see 1 Peter 1:20), Arminians rightly protest that if this is true in Romans 8:29, then Paul teaches that those whom God chose ("foreknew") he also chose ("predestined"). But I do not think that Paul is simply repeating the same idea. How shall we decide the meaning of foreknowledge here? Our approach will be to survey the meanings of "know" in Scripture, to consider the uses of "foreknow" and "foreknowledge," and then to address the meaning of "foreknew" in Romans 8:29.

"Know," "Foreknow," and "Foreknowledge" in Scripture. The word "know" has a broad range of meanings in Scripture. In the Old Testament the word *yada'* means: "know, learn to know" something, for example, "good and evil" (Gen. 3:22); "know a person," whether a human being (Gen. 29:5) or God himself (Ex. 5:2); "know someone" with sexual knowledge (Gen. 4:1); "know how to do" something, such as hunt (Gen. 25:27) or play a lyre (1 Sam. 16:16); and "have knowledge, be wise" (Eccl. 9:11).[5] The range of meanings for "to know" (*ginōskō*) is equally broad in the New Testament: "know" a person (for example, God, Rom. 1:21); "learn of" a situation (Col. 4:8); "understand" the parables (Mark 4:13); "perceive" wickedness (Matt. 22:18); as a euphemism for "sexual relations" (Matt. 1:25); "have come to know" a person (John 1:48); and "acknowledge" that which one is or claims to be (Matt. 7:23).[6]

The words "foreknow" and "foreknowledge" do not occur in the Old Testament and are used only five times in the apocryphal books, written between the Testaments. The words have a range of meaning, including prescience, the knowing of facts beforehand (Wisd. of Sol. 8:8; 18:6; Jth. 11:19), personal knowledge (of wisdom personified, Wisd. of Sol. 6:13), and God's planning (Jth. 9:6). "Foreknow" and "foreknowledge" appear seven times in the New Testament and signify the following: knowing a person and

5. F. Brown, S. Driver, and C. Briggs, יָדַע (*yada'*), in *The Brown-Driver-Briggs Hebrew and English Lexicon* (Peabody, MA: Hendrickson, 2005), 393.

6. William F. Arndt and F. Wilbur Gingrich, γινώσκω (*ginōskō*), in *A Greek–English Lexicon of the New Testament and Other Early Christian Literature*, ed. F. Wilbur Gingrich and Fredrick W. Danker, revised and augmented from Walter Bauer's 5th ed. (Chicago: University of Chicago Press, 1979), 160–61.

his way of life for a long time (Acts 26:5); knowing facts before-hand (2 Peter 3:17); God's knowing Christ (1 Peter 1:20) and his crucifixion (Acts 2:23), which both involve God's intention; God's foreknowing his people (Rom. 8:29; 11:2; 1 Peter 1:1–2).

"Foreknew" in Romans 8:29. With this background we are prepared to address the meaning of "foreknew" in Romans 8:29: "For those whom he foreknew he also predestined." The combi-nation of words is very important. Romans 8:29 corresponds to passages in which a person knows or foreknows other persons. In this case, God is the person who foreknows his people. This parallels other passages in which God or Christ knows persons in a saving relationship. Listen to Jesus' words condemning hypocrites: "I never knew you; depart from me, you workers of lawlessness" (Matt. 7:23). Jesus does not mean that he was ig-norant of certain facts; instead, he means that he did not know the hypocrites with the knowledge of salvation. Similarly, Jesus' announcement, "I am the good shepherd. I know my own and my own know me" (John 10:14), does not speak primarily of facts, but of a saving relationship. In terms of facts, he knows both sheep and goats completely. But he does not know both with the knowledge of salvation.

Paul's words to the Galatians also conform to the pattern of a person's knowing other persons: "Formerly, when you did not know God, you were enslaved to those that by nature are not gods. But now . . . *you have come to know God*, or rather *to be known by God*" (Gal. 4:8–9). Here Paul does not tell of the Galatians' know-ing of information, but of their knowing a person—God—and of God's knowing them.

As previously noted, "foreknow" at times refers to someone's knowing facts beforehand, but that is not its meaning in Romans 8:29. Although it is true that God knows all facts, Paul does not say here that God knows certain facts, such as whether people would believe the gospel or not. Rather, Paul says that God foreknows certain people, and the meaning of "foreknow" is thus similar to that of "know" in Matthew 7:23, John 10:14, and Galatians

111

4:8–9—it speaks of God having a saving relationship with people. I. Howard Marshall agrees concerning "foreknow" in Romans 8:29: "It is generally agreed that the 'knowing' in this verb must be understood in the Hebraic sense of fixing one's loving regard upon a person."[7]

Those three passages contain the word "know," whereas Romans 8:29 has "foreknow." The difference is that the former passages speak of God knowing people and the latter one of him knowing them beforehand. When Paul writes that "God foreknew" his people in Romans 8:29, then, he means that God planned to set his love upon them, to enter into a saving personal relationship with them. If we inquire when this took place, we learn from the teaching of other Scriptures that God did this "before the foundation of the world" (Eph. 1:4) and "before the ages began" (2 Tim. 1:9). We conclude that when Paul wrote, "For those whom he foreknew he also predestined," he meant that "God predestines us on the basis of his gracious commitment to us before the world was."[8] God loved people and chose them for salvation before creation.

Does this mean that God loved everyone and chose them all for salvation? We must answer in the negative because of the way the five verbs are interconnected. Those foreknown are the same ones who are predestined, called, justified, and glorified. Because it is clear that not everyone will be glorified, it follows that not everyone is foreknown or loved beforehand.

Arminian Approaches

How do Arminians deal with this passage? One might ascertain at least four ways. First, they sometimes neglect it. H. Orton Wiley makes no mention of it when he treats predestination in his three-volume *Christian Theology*.[9] H. Ray Dunning in his 671-

---

7. I. Howard Marshall, *Kept by the Power of God: A Study of Perseverance and Falling Away* (London: Epworth Press, 1969), 93.

8. S. M. Baugh, "The Meaning of Foreknowledge," in *Still Sovereign: Contemporary Perspectives on Election, Foreknowledge, and Grace*, ed. Thomas R. Schreiner and Bruce A. Ware (Grand Rapids: Baker, 2000), 194.

9. H. Orton Wiley, *Christian Theology*, 3 vols. (Kansas City: Beacon Hill, 1969), 2:335–40.

page systematic theology says only, "Paul makes this clear in that concatenation of election concepts in Romans 8:28–29. The ultimate purpose for which God chooses (predestines and elects) His people is that they 'be conformed to the image of his Son.'"[10] Of course, that is true, but the passage has much more to teach concerning election. Avoidance of key passages is no way to deal with the Bible's teaching.

Second, Arminians commonly interpret Romans 8:29, "For those whom he foreknew he also predestined," to mean that God predestines people to salvation based on his foresight of their repentance and faith in the gospel. Grant Osborne summarizes: "In every aspect foreknowledge and election are two aspects of divine predestination. God's sovereign choice always takes into consideration the free will of the individual."[11]

But neither here nor elsewhere does the Bible say that God chose people for salvation based on his foreknowing of their faith or unbelief. Rather, as Steven Baugh aptly says:

> The classic Arminian interpretation of Romans 8:29, that God's foreknowledge of faith is in view, is clearly reading one's theology into the text. Paul does not say: "whose faith he foreknew," but "whom he foreknew." He foreknew us. . . . But in Romans 8:29, predestination is not dependent on faith; rather, God predestines us on the basis of his gracious commitment to us before the world was.[12]

Third, Ken Grider interprets Romans 8:29–30 as speaking of "temporal predestination." He explains: "Predestination does not have to do with a pre-decision of God regarding the eternal destiny of people, but . . . it has to do with what God graciously

10. H. Ray Dunning, *Grace, Faith and Holiness: A Wesleyan Systematic Theology* (Kansas City: Beacon Hill Press, 1988), 508.

11. Grant Osborne, "Exegetical Notes on Calvinist Texts," in *Grace Unlimited*, 178. Cf. Roger T. Forster and V. Paul Marston, *God's Strategy in Human History* (Wheaton: Tyndale House, 1973), 101. Ken Grider agrees: "This passage states that 'those God foreknew,' meaning surely those He foreknew would believe." J. Kenneth Grider, *A Wesleyan-Holiness Theology* (Kansas City: Beacon Hill Press, 1994), 250.

12. Baugh, "The Meaning of Foreknowledge," 194.

decides for believers temporally."[13] After affirming that predestination in Romans 8:29 results in believers being conformed to Christ's likeness, he writes, "The point here, however, is that eternal destiny does not enter into the picture at all—except as an ultimate consequence of the success or failure of this predestination."[14] But conformity to Christ *is* the eternal destiny of Christians. Therefore, when Paul writes, "Those whom he foreknew he also predestined to be conformed to the image of his Son" (Rom. 8:29), he teaches that predestination is unto the eternal destiny of conformity to Christ. Election also results in final salvation expressed as glorification, as the passage teaches: "For those whom he . . . predestined to be conformed to the image of his Son . . . he also glorified" (vv. 29–30).

Fourth, Arminians have sometimes assumed conditions of human faith when reading Romans 8:29–30. Grider attempts (as John Wesley did) to loosen the links in the chain of the five verbs in Romans 8:29–30: "So, in Romans 8:30, God *foresees that individuals will believe*; and in due time He calls them to himself in various ways, as through preaching and by the Spirit's summons. And *as they respond favorably* to this call, He justifies them. Then, *still based on His foreknowledge* (see v. 29) *that individuals will keep on believing*, He glorifies them."[15] The italicized words signify Grider's additions to the biblical text, added in an attempt to harmonize Paul's words with the Arminian doctrine of conditional election.

But there are no breaks in the chain of verbs. Paul uses a literary device called "climax," brought out well by the NASB: "For *whom* He foreknew, He also predestined . . . ; and *whom* He predestined, *these* He also called; and *whom* He called, *these* He also justified; and *whom* He justified, *these* He also glorified" (Rom. 8:29–30).[16] Paul's construction (marked in italics) "identify-

13. Grider, *A Wesleyan-Holiness Theology*, 249. Cf. Osborne, "Exegetical Notes on Calvinist Texts," 178.
14. Grider, *A Wesleyan-Holiness Theology*, 251.
15. Ibid. Cf. Walls and Dongell, *Why I Am Not a Calvinist*, 83 (italics added).
16. This citation is from the 1977 edition of the New American Standard Bible. Cf. the American Standard Version and Holman Christian Standard Bible.

ing the objects of one divine initiative as the objects of the next pounds a drumbeat through the text. With this rhetorical device of 'climax' Paul posits a continuity in the beneficiaries of salvation from its first manifestation in God's eternal counsel to its final one in glorification."[17] Paul does not make salvation contingent on human faithfulness, but on divine grace from beginning to end. When Arminians add conditions to Paul's words to make the passage better fit their theology, they change the meaning of the apostle's words.

Romans 9:6–24

Let us consider Romans 9:6–24, the Bible's most famous election passage, in its historical context. That context concerns Paul's exhortations to unity addressed to two factions in the church at Rome: the weak and the strong believers. Who were the weak believers? They were Jewish Christians who kept a kosher table (Rom. 14:2, 14) and kept Jewish religious days in addition to Sunday (v. 5). Who were the strong believers? They were the Gentile Christians whose consciences enabled them to eat anything and to reject the observance of Jewish festivals. Paul's message to both factions in the church at Rome is straightforward: "So then let us pursue what makes for peace and for mutual upbuilding. . . . Therefore welcome one another as Christ has welcomed you, for the glory of God" (Rom. 14:19; 15:7).

This background enables us to better understand Paul's frequent mention in Romans of the "Jew" and the "Gentile" (Rom. 1:16; 2:9, 10; 3:9, 29; 9:24; 10:12). One purpose of the epistle is to promote unity in a church that is ethnically divided between Jews and Gentiles. Considered in light of the historical background, Romans 9, 10, and 11 are not parenthetical chapters, as is sometimes thought, but are the section of Romans most focused on bringing healing to a divided congregation.

17. Judith M. Gundry Volf, *Paul and Perseverance: Staying In and Falling Away* (Louisville: Westminster John Knox Press, 1990), 14.

The Jewish Christians in Rome have a problem. They were among the pilgrims at Pentecost when the New Testament church began (Acts 2:10–11). Their congregation, as with every local church at the beginning, is Jewish Christian. But by the time the apostle writes the book of Romans, the Jewish Christians in Rome are a minority in the church they founded (Rom. 11:13). Moreover, their Gentile brothers and sisters do not always treat them with respect (Rom. 14:1, 4, 10, 13, 15, 19). As a result, the Jewish Christians are struggling with a key question: have God's promises to Israel failed?

A Troubling Question

After reviewing the great blessings that God showered upon Israel, Paul addresses the issue troubling the Jews: "It is not as though the word of God has failed" (Rom. 9:6). Paul answers that question in three chapters. First, he replies that God's word did not fail but that he did exactly what he planned to do in his sovereignty (9:6–29). Second, he answers the same question in terms of human freedom: God's word has not failed; but because Israel refused to believe in the Lord, he rejected the nation (9:30–10:21). Third, Paul replies in terms of God's faithfulness to his promises made to the patriarchs: God will still convert a Jewish remnant (11:1–32).

God's Promise Has Not Failed

Our main concern is with chapter 9. To assure the Jewish Christians in Rome that God's promise to Israel has not failed (Rom. 9:6), Paul gives a lesson in redemptive history. From the beginning, God has sovereignly fulfilled his word to Israel, despite the people's lack of faith and waywardness.

God accomplishes his plan by giving Abraham and Sarah an heir (Rom. 9:6–9). Physical descent from Abraham is not by itself enough to establish membership in Israel, a line of descent that comes through Abraham and Sarah's son, Isaac. "It is not the children of the flesh who are the children of God, but the children of *the promise* are counted as offspring" (v. 8). Does "the promise" here refer to the gospel, as it sometimes does in Paul? Does "the promise" refer to God's calling on people to believe? No, for Paul tells what promise he had in mind: "For this is what the promise said: 'About this time next year I will return and Sarah shall have a son'" (v. 9). The promise is God's sovereign declaration that an infertile couple will have a son. Previously, Abraham and Sarah had taken matters into their own hands, in accordance with ancient Near Eastern custom, by using Sarah's handmaid, Hagar, to produce Ishmael. But God would not fulfill his promise through Abraham and Sarah's scheming. Rather, he would grant the child of promise using a man whose "body . . . was as good as dead" and his wife, whose womb was barren (Rom. 4:19). God's word has not failed; he sovereignly fulfills it against all human striving.

God also displays his reign in the next generation (Rom. 9:10–13). The twins Jacob and Esau had the same father, Isaac. And Esau, not Jacob, was the firstborn. Nevertheless, God chose Jacob over Esau. In fact, "though they were not yet born and had done nothing either good or bad—in order that God's purpose of election might continue, not because of works but because of his call—she [Rebecca, their mother] was told, 'The older will serve the younger.' As it is written, 'Jacob I loved, but Esau I hated'" (vv. 11–13). This scenario played out according to a divine plan, not a human one. God chose the second son, Jacob, over the firstborn, Esau, to draw attention to his sovereign "purpose of election" (v. 11).

Two Protests

The words of Paul's imaginary protester in Romans 9:14 substantiate our treatment of verses 6–13: "What shall we say then? Is there injustice on God's part?" The apostle would not reply to the protester as he does if God had based predestination on his foreknowing human response to the gospel. Paul could have said, "I am glad you made that protest because it

117

indicates that you mistook my meaning. I do not mean that God is utterly sovereign in human affairs. He does not choose us without taking our free will into account. Instead, he ratifies our choice of him." But Paul responds to the objector in this way: "By no means! For he says to Moses, 'I will have mercy on whom I have mercy, and I will have compassion on whom I have compassion'" (vv. 14c–15). Rather than backing away from the idea of God's strong sovereignty implied by the objector, Paul underscores it. God is free to have mercy on whomever he wills. What is determinative in matters pertaining to salvation is not our will but God's will.

The next verse is very difficult to reconcile with an Arminian understanding of salvation: "So then it depends not on human will or exertion, but on God, who has mercy" (v. 16). Arminianism teaches that God gives grace to everyone and that the determining factor in salvation is what we do with grace. Yet Paul explicitly excludes human desire (literally, "willing") and effort (literally, "running") as determining factors. God is the determining factor in salvation, not human beings' responses.

God's dealings with Pharaoh confirm our interpretation of the passage so far. Although it would be appropriate for Paul to mention Pharaoh's hardening of his heart in Romans 10, where he speaks of human freedom, he does not do so here. Instead, he affirms that God raised up Pharaoh in order to demonstrate God's power and glory among the nations (v. 17). Paul brings his redemptive-history lesson, begun in Romans 9:6, to a conclusion that demolishes theologies grounded in free will: "So then he has mercy on whomever he wills, and he hardens whomever he wills" (v. 18). In verse 15, Paul had said that God is sovereign in his showing mercy and compassion. Now he goes one step further: God is sovereign both in his showing mercy and in his hardening.

In Romans 9:19, similar to verse 14, Paul brings up a protest to his strong teaching that God is completely sovereign in salvation: "You will say to me then, 'Why does he still find fault? For who can resist his will?'" In response to this objection, Paul does not qualify his emphasis on God's absolute sovereignty. Rather, he replies: "But who are you, O man, to answer back to God? Will what is molded say to its molder, 'Why have you made me like this?'" (v. 20). If the Arminian understanding of predestination were correct, here would be an ideal place for Paul to say so: "Your objection shows that you have misunderstood me. I do not mean that God utterly controls salvation. Rather, he always takes our free will into account. Election means that he ratifies our choice of him. If we did not have a part, it would be unjust of God to still find fault with us. If we cannot resist the will of the Almighty, then he treats us unfairly." But Paul says none of this. Instead, he puts us in our place, far below the high and holy, great and awesome, sovereign and incomprehensible God: "But who are you, O man, to answer back to God?" Paul teaches that God's creatures, including human beings, have no ultimate right to hold him accountable to our understanding of eternal things. No, it is he—almighty God—who holds us accountable. It is he—not puny human creatures—who has the ultimate say in matters of eternal destinies.

Paul is not finished with his imaginary objector: "Has the potter no right over the clay, to make out of the same lump one vessel for honored use and another for dishonorable use?" (v. 21). As the Greek implies, Paul expects a positive answer to this question.[18] God, the divine Potter, can do as he pleases with the pots that he fashions from a lump of clay. Again, the apostle underlines God's prerogative in doing what he wants with his human creatures.

Paul next uses a rhetorical question to give the Bible's strongest teaching on election: "What if God, desiring to show his wrath and to make known his power, has endured with much patience vessels of wrath prepared for destruction, in order to make known the riches of his glory for vessels of mercy, which he has prepared beforehand for glory?" (vv. 22–23). Paul seems to teach that God stands behind the fate of every human being,

---

18. Paul uses the negative particle οὐκ (*ouk*) in a question.

whether for glory or wrath. But does the apostle really teach double predestination in these verses?

Arminian Strategies

Arminian scholars do not think so. They employ five main strategies to deal with these verses. First, they commonly ignore them. This is true for the standard Arminian systematic theologies of Orton Wiley, Ray Dunning, and Ken Grider. When they treat predestination, they neglect Romans 9:6–24.

Second, Arminians suggest that Paul's long question in verses 22–23 is hypothetical. When the apostle asks, "What if God . . . ?" he merely states a hypothesis.

> While the passage [Rom. 9:6–29] affirms God's right as a sovereign Creator to deal with any and all of His creatures in whatever manner He pleases, either for good or for ill, without becoming answerable to any man, . . . quite to the contrary, . . . God is governed by His desire to have mercy on all and takes full account of men's response to His overtures of grace and calls to repentance.[19]

Third, Arminians sometimes assert that Paul is not treating salvation in these verses, but the historical destiny of nations, especially Israel. Forster and Marston, for example, write: "The question at issue is not the eternal destiny of anyone, but the history of Israel and their significance as the chosen nation."[20]

Fourth, Clark Pinnock is representative of many who claim that Romans 9 deals with election to corporate salvation, not individual salvation.[21]

Fifth, Jerry Walls and Joseph Dongell argue that Calvinists have read their theology of God's sovereignty into these verses

19. Robert Shank, *Elect in the Son: A Study of the Doctrine of Election* (Springfield, MO: Westcott Publishers, 1970), 188. See also pp. 174, 194.
20. Roger T. Forster and V. Paul Marston, *God's Strategy in Human History* (Wheaton, IL: Tyndale House, 1973), 67.
21. Clark H. Pinnock, "From Augustine to Arminius: A Pilgrimage in Theology," in *The Grace of God, the Will of Man*, ed. Clark H. Pinnock (Grand Rapids: Zondervan, 1989), 20.

instead of paying close attention to Paul's argument in Romans 9. They claim that if the verses are read in light of the whole of Romans 9–11, it can be seen that Paul never intended to teach unconditional individual election to salvation and damnation. Rather, "God has a sovereign right, insists Paul, to condition the salvation of individual Israelites upon their faith, however deeply this may offend their sense of entitlement based on their racial connection to Abraham."[22]

Reply to Arminian Strategies

I will reply to the five Arminian strategies. First, to neglect Romans 9:6–23 in a study of election is irresponsible, since this is the major biblical passage on the subject.

Second, Paul commonly uses rhetorical questions as teaching devices, including in the three verses immediately preceding Romans 9:22–24—verses 19, 20, and 21. And Paul's question here is not hypothetical but rhetorical: "What if God, desiring to show his wrath and to make known his power, has endured with much patience vessels of wrath prepared for destruction, in order to make known the riches of his glory for vessels of mercy, which he has prepared beforehand for glory—*even us whom he has called, not from the Jews only but also from the Gentiles?*" (vv. 22–24). Paul's question is not hypothetical because he includes many first-century Jews and Gentiles among the "vessels of mercy."

Third, Paul is not treating the historical destiny of Israel but salvation, as Thomas Schreiner has shown: "When Paul speaks of the anguish in his heart and his desire to be accursed because of his fellow Israelites (Rom. 9:1–3), he feels this way not because Israel is merely losing out on temporal blessings. Distress torments his heart because his kinsmen from Israel were not saved."[23]

Fourth, the claim that Romans 9 deals with election to corporate salvation and not to individual salvation does not hold up

---

22. Walls and Dongell, *Why I Am Not a Calvinist*, 92.
23. Thomas R. Schreiner, "Does Romans 9 Teach Individual Election unto Salvation?" in *Still Sovereign*, 91. Schreiner gives four good arguments, of which this is the first.

to biblical scrutiny, for Paul speaks of both here, as Schreiner has successfully argued:

> Evidence that individual election is also in Paul's mind is found in Romans 9:15, where he cites Exodus 33:19: "I will have mercy on whom I have mercy, and I will have compassion on whom I have compassion." The word whom (*hon*) is singular, indicating that specific individuals upon whom God has mercy are in view . . .
> The selection of a remnant out of Israel (Rom. 9:6–9; 11:1–6) also involves the selecting out of certain individuals from a larger group.[24]

Fifth, Arminians do the very thing that Walls and Dongell accuse Calvinists of doing with these verses. They read their theology of human free will into Romans 9 in spite of the strong words of that chapter. Where does Romans 9 teach that God conditions the salvation of persons on foreseen faith? Nowhere. Rather, Paul repeatedly insists that salvation is the free gift of almighty God, and that he gives to whomever he wants. God has mercy on whom he wants and has compassion on whom he wants (v. 15). Salvation "depends *not* on human will or exertion, but on God, who has mercy" (v. 16). God shows mercy on whom he wills to show mercy, and he hardens whom he wills (v. 18). And God puts in their place any who question his right to do what he wants with his own creatures (vv. 19–21)!

God the Creator, Paul affirms, holds divine prerogatives over his creatures. The "vessels of mercy" are those whom God has chosen for glory, and the "vessels of wrath" are those whom God passes over and thereby appoints for judgment.

Conclusion

These three most famous passages on election are big rocks on which the ship of Arminian teaching on predestination found-

24. Ibid., 99. Once more Schreiner advances more good arguments than the two that I cite.

ers. Although Arminianism holds that election is corporate rather than individual, in Romans 9 Paul affirms that it is both individual and corporate: God chose Jacob and not Esau (vv. 10–13). He also chose individuals to constitute the corporate entity of the Christian church (vv. 19–24). The people predestined and glorified in Romans 8:29–30 are a group but do not include all humanity. Therefore, this group is made up of many individuals and excludes other individuals. In Ephesians 1, those chosen from among the Jews (v. 12) and Gentiles (v. 13) constitute the Christian church, but since not all human beings will be saved, the group of those chosen is made up of some individuals but not all.

Furthermore, the Arminian view that election is for service and not salvation does not square with Romans 9. God's election has the result that people receive his gift of salvation viewed as mercy (Rom. 9:15–16, 18, 23) and as glory (v. 23). In Romans 8, God's predestination of his people results in their being conformed to Christ and glorified (vv. 29–30). And in Ephesians 1, God chose and predestined us to final sanctification (v. 4) and adoption (v. 5). Service is not in view in these passages, but of course election results in both salvation and service, as Romans 12–16 and Ephesians 4–6 attest.

The Arminian doctrine that God bases election on foreseen human faith cuts across the grain of Romans 9, for Paul expressly excludes human willing in salvation: "So then it depends not on *human will* or exertion, but on God, who has mercy" (Rom. 9:16). In addition, Paul presents the positive basis of predestination as divine and not human—it is God's love (v. 13), mercy (vv. 15, 16, 18, 23), compassion (v. 15), and sovereign will (vv. 19–24). It is the same for Romans 8, where Paul says not that God foreknew people's response to the gospel, but that he foreknew (foreloved) his own (Rom. 8:29) and predestined them for calling, justification, and glorification (vv. 29–30). And Ephesians 1 also does not base predestination on foreseen human repentance and faith, but on God's love (Eph. 1:4, 6) and sovereignty (vv. 5, 11).

How shall we respond to the message that God has chosen us for salvation? By blessing God the Father, "who has blessed us . . . , even as he chose us in him [Christ] before the foundation of the world" (Eph. 1:3–4). By exulting in "the praise of his glorious grace" (v. 6). By living "to the praise of" the "glory" of God almighty, who "predestined" us "according to" his purpose and "who works all things according to the counsel of his will" (vv. 11–12).

How can God's election help embattled Christians, such as those in Rome (see Rom. 8:18–23, 35–37)? It should give them confidence that nothing is out of their strong and loving heavenly Father's control. They can know that "for those who love God all things work together for good, for those who are called according to his purpose" (Rom. 8:28). This is why they can be sure of this: Paul assures them of final conformity to Christ and glorification because God predestined them for both (Rom. 8:29–30).

Moreover, the Romans, especially the Jewish believers, needed to be assured that God's word had not failed (Rom. 9:6). Not only has he ruled again and again in redemptive history (vv. 7–18), but he has also ruled in calling sinners to himself in salvation in Rome, both Jews and Gentiles (v. 24). Those called were previously "vessels of mercy, which he has prepared beforehand for glory" (v. 23). He who called them is the sovereign Creator who exercises divine prerogatives over his creatures (vv. 19–23). Because salvation "depends not on human will or exertion, but on God, who has mercy" (v. 16), sinners saved by grace can have great confidence that "there is therefore now no condemnation for those who are in Christ Jesus" (Rom. 8:1). Indeed, God wants them to be assured that nothing "will be able to separate" them "from the love of God in Christ Jesus our Lord" (v. 39).

Free Will

So far we have focused on God's election of his people for salvation because election is the book's primary subject. But to ignore human free will would be inexcusable. Divine sovereignty, and predestination that flows from it, must be viewed alongside human freedom, and faith in Christ that flows from it. Otherwise, distortion will result.

It takes looking at something, or someone, from multiple perspectives to gain a full appreciation. Consider Albert Pujols, the St. Louis Cardinals first baseman and hitting phenom. People who follow baseball know that Pujols has put up unprecedented batting numbers in his first five years in the big leagues. But many do not know that he has established a foundation to help children with Down syndrome, like his daughter Isabella, and to aid impoverished children in Albert's native Dominican Republic. And relatively few have heard his testimony as an evangelical Christian.

> Albert shares; "Growing up in the Dominican Republic, I lived to play baseball. My wife Deidre, who was my girlfriend at the time, shared how much Jesus loved me. I realized I needed more than religion. I needed a Savior. Jesus Christ wanted a personal relationship with me."
>
> On November 13, 1998 Albert made what he calls "The best decision of my life." He gave his heart to Jesus Christ and asked him to become the Lord of his life.[1]

1. Pujols Family Foundation, "About Our Faith," http://www.pujolsfamilyfoundation.org/faith.htm.

The important matter of the freedom of the will is also best explored from more than one perspective. Here we will consider three:

- Free Will and the Bible's Story
- Free Will and the Reasons Why People Are Saved and Condemned
- Free Will and Its Relation to God's Sovereignty

Free Will and the Bible's Story

In order to think biblically about the freedom that people possess, we must ask a crucial question: where are those persons located in the biblical story? Human freedom looks different at the various times human beings appear in the story: at creation, as fallen people after the fall, as redeemed people after the fall, and as glorified people after the resurrection of the dead.

Human Beings as Created Had True Freedom and Freedom of Choice

God, the Creator of the heavens and the earth, bestowed marvelous freedom on Adam and Eve. In order to appreciate that freedom, we must make an important distinction—between freedom of choice and what we will call true freedom. *Freedom of choice* is the ability of human beings to do as they wish, and for that reason it is also called the freedom of spontaneity. Adam and Eve, in fact all human beings, are created free to make choices based on their inclinations.

Some are surprised to hear that Adam and Eve's true freedom did not consist in freedom of choice alone. *True freedom* is more than freedom of choice or spontaneity. Because God made Adam and Eve for himself, he made them to know, love, and serve him and each other. True freedom, therefore, is not merely the freedom to make spontaneous choices; it is also freedom of relationship with God—the ability to know, love, serve, and enjoy

126

him—and with other human beings. God created Adam and Eve for relationship with himself (Gen. 1:26–27). Adam and Eve did not say, "Who is *that* walking in the garden?" (Gen. 3:8), for they *knew* the Lord God as their Lord and God (Gen. 2:7, 21–23).

The true freedom in which our first parents were created did not last, however, for they believed the devil's lie and wanted to become like God. They ate the forbidden fruit, fell from original righteousness, and marred their beautiful relationship with God and each other (Gen. 3:6–8). Although they retained freedom of choice, their true freedom was lost. So when people ask whether human beings have freedom, we must ask what they mean by "freedom" and what point in biblical history they are talking about. Freedom of choice or spontaneity? Always. True freedom, freedom of relationship with God and fellow human beings? It was lost in the fall.[2]

Human Beings as Fallen Lost True Freedom and Retained Freedom of Choice

The greatest transition in the whole story occurs in Genesis 3. There, because Adam and Eve sinned, Paradise was lost and the painful effects of the fall were introduced. Original sin includes both original guilt and original pollution. *Original guilt* is the truth that because of Adam's sin we all are guilty, a truth that Paul underscores in Romans 5: "For the judgment following one trespass brought condemnation. . . . Therefore, . . . one trespass led to condemnation for all men" (Rom. 5:16b, 18).[3] This is a far cry from the original true freedom of a loving and enjoyable relationship with God; now our first parents stood guilty before him.

Original pollution (or, as it is also called, original corruption) means that our lives and relationships are stained by sin. As a

---

2. I gratefully acknowledge a debt to Robert A. Pyne, professor of theological studies, Dallas Theological Seminary, for some of the ideas in this section and for his helpful comments on this chapter.

3. Another text that teaches original sin is Ephesians 2:3: "We . . . were by nature children of wrath, like the rest of mankind."

result of Adam's fall, our thoughts and words are displeasing to God (Jer. 17:9; James 3:6). Sin comes from within, from hearts that are corrupt and polluted (Mark 7:21–23). Although we commit actual sins, for which we are justly condemned, the root of our problem goes back to Adam and his primal sin. We retain freedom of choice, but the inclination of our will is no longer to love and serve God, but to rebel against him. True freedom has been lost.

The key aspect of original pollution for this chapter is *inability*. Adam's sin causes us to be enslaved to sin and unable to rescue ourselves. At least four passages teach inability: John 6:44, 65; John 8:34, 36; 1 Corinthians 2:14–15; and 2 Corinthians 4:3–4. According to these passages, one of the effects of the original pollution of Adam's fall is that sinners are unable even to believe the gospel on their own. Arminianism and Calvinism have different views of inability. Arminianism holds that although sinners are unable to believe on their own, none of them are actually on their own. Rather, because God gives prevenient (preparing) grace[4] to every human being, no one is actually unable to believe. Calvinists disagree and hold that inability is not hypothetical, as Arminians maintain, but actual.

Jesus was not speaking hypothetically but was describing the actual condition of his unbelieving hearers when he said, "No one can come to me unless the Father who sent me draws him" (John 6:44) and "Everyone who commits sin is a slave to sin" (John 8:34). Likewise, Paul was not speaking theoretically but was describing what happens when the gospel is preached when he said: "The man without the Spirit does not accept the things that come from the Spirit of God, . . . and he cannot understand them" (1 Cor. 2:14 NIV), and "The god of this age has blinded the minds of unbelievers, so that they cannot see the light of the gospel" (2 Cor. 4:4 NIV). We conclude, then, that the Calvinist doctrine of inability is

---

4. Prevenient grace is God's grace that precedes salvation. According to Calvinism, it actually accomplishes salvation for the elect; according to Arminianism, it makes possible salvation for all.

correct and that one of the results of the fall is that lost persons are bound in sin and unable to trust Christ on their own.[5]

Although human beings always have freedom of choice, as the result of Adam's sin and our own, the inclination of our will (apart from Christ) is not to glorify God but to glorify ourselves. We thus use the retained freedom of spontaneity to sin against our Maker and fellow human beings. In sin we have lost the true freedom of relationship with God and do not naturally know, love, and serve him as our first parents did before the fall. In short, though we still have freedom of choice, we have lost the true freedom of relationship with God and one another. And to make matters worse, we are enslaved by our sin and unable to rescue ourselves.

Human Beings as Redeemed Have Regained a Measure of True Freedom and Retained Freedom of Choice

At this seemingly hopeless point, the Bible has good news for us:

> For while we were still weak, at the right time Christ died for the ungodly. For one will scarcely die for a righteous person—though perhaps for a good person one would dare even to die—but God shows his love for us in that while we were still sinners, Christ died for us. (Rom. 5:6–8)

When we were helpless and unable to rescue ourselves from the domain of sin, God stepped in and sent his Son on the greatest rescue mission. God "has delivered us from the domain of darkness and transferred us to the kingdom of his beloved Son, in whom we have redemption, the forgiveness of sins" (Col. 1:13–14). As a result, sin's stranglehold on our lives is broken and we again enjoy a measure of true freedom.

Jesus taught this doctrine in John 8, as we have seen. For, after warning, "Truly, truly, I say to you, everyone who commits

5. For more argumentation, see Robert A. Peterson and Michael D. Williams, *Why I Am Not an Arminian* (Downers Grove, IL: InterVarsity Press, 2004), 162–72.

sin is a slave to sin," he assured his hearers, "So if the Son sets you free, you will be free indeed" (John 8:34, 36). By the grace of God, believers in Christ are once again able to love, serve, and enjoy God, much as Adam and Eve did before the fall. Paul, too, rejoices that "for freedom Christ has set us free; stand firm, therefore, and do not submit again to a yoke of slavery" (Gal. 5:1).

The verse just quoted illustrates well a point made by Anthony Hoekema—true freedom is both a gift of God and a task of human beings:

> Though it is God who restores our true freedom in the redemptive process, the exercise of that freedom also involves human responsibility. . . . To begin with, then, human beings must turn to Christ in faith in order to receive true freedom. Though they cannot turn to Christ apart from the enabling power of the Holy Spirit, yet they must so turn. . . . The continued exercise of our true freedom also involves our responsibility. . . . We cannot live as free men and women without God's help, but nevertheless we must do so. Our true freedom is not only a gift; it is also a task.[6]

The gift and task of true freedom are intertwined in Paul's famous passage on Christian freedom in Romans 6:6, 14, 17–18, 22.

This freedom is not to be confused with sinless perfection. John makes this clear: "If we say we have no sin, we deceive ourselves, and the truth is not in us. . . . If we say we have not sinned, we make him a liar, and his word is not in us" (1 John 1:8, 10). Godly Christians who have walked with the Lord for years are more aware of their sinfulness than when they first came to Christ. What is the antidote to the poison of ongoing sin in the Christian life? "If we confess our sins, he is faithful and just to forgive us our sins and to cleanse us from all unrighteousness" (1 John 1:9). The antidote is heartfelt confession and acceptance of forgiveness and cleansing from Christ.

6. Anthony A. Hoekema, *Created in God's Image* (Grand Rapids: Eerdmans, 1986), 236–37.

Nevertheless, sinless perfection is the goal that every believer in Christ will attain in future glory.

In Christ, then, the freedom of positive relationship with God is restored; we know God and are enabled by the Holy Spirit to love and serve him and one another. The Spirit gives us new inclinations of the will, but our old sinful inclinations still haunt us. We want to glorify God—and do much of the time—but we still live selfishly and fail to glorify him. Consequently, although we have recovered much of the true freedom lost in the fall, we "groan inwardly as we wait eagerly for adoption as sons, the redemption of our bodies" (Rom. 8:23). Perfect, true freedom still awaits those who have been saved by Christ.

Human Beings as Glorified Will Be Perfected in True Freedom and Will Retain Freedom of Choice

The goal of our salvation is glorification and complete sanctification in the presence of God on the renewed earth. True freedom will be perfected only after the resurrection of the dead. On that day we will know, love, and enjoy God and fellow believers as Adam and Eve did before the fall. "The throne of God and of the Lamb will be in it [the New Jerusalem], and his servants will worship him" (Rev. 22:3). What will be their occupation? "Therefore they are before the throne of God, and serve him day and night in his temple" (Rev. 7:15).

In fact, things will be even better than they were before the fall because, unlike Adam and Eve, as "the spirits of the righteous made perfect" (Heb. 12:23) we will not be able to sin. This truth is instructive in light of the idea that the epitome of true freedom is the ability to choose between righteousness and sin. It is not. *True freedom is the ability to love and serve God unhindered by sin.* Of course, we will still have freedom of choice after we are resurrected and perfected, but having only God-honoring inclinations of the will, we will want only to glorify and please God, and we will enjoy him forever.

131

Conclusion

It is fruitful to consider human freedom in light of the unfolding biblical story. At creation God gave Adam and Eve freedom of choice and true freedom. Freedom of choice is the ability to make spontaneous choices according to the inclinations of the will. This is an unlosable part of our humanness. By contrast, true freedom is losable, and in fact was lost in the fall. True freedom is relational; it is the ability to know, love, serve, and enjoy God as he intended.

Because of Adam's original sin in the garden of Eden, human beings lost true freedom. Although we retain freedom of choice, we are guilty before a holy and just God (original guilt) and our lives are defiled by sin (original pollution). The most damaging effect of sin on human freedom is inability. Because of Adam's sin and our own sins, we are unable to rescue ourselves from sin. Fallen human beings are unable on their own even to trust Christ as Lord and Savior (John 6:44, 65; 1 Cor. 2:14–15; 2 Cor. 4:3–4). They desperately need the Spirit of God to work in their hearts.

When the Spirit does work, persons come to know Christ. The Spirit regenerates them, overcoming their spiritual deadness and making them alive to God. In so doing, God restores to them a measure of true freedom. Like Adam and Eve in the garden, Christians know, love, and serve God, at least to some degree. But sin remains in them, and they do not love him with all their hearts. Instead, still having evil inclinations, they sin and must regularly seek forgiveness to enjoy God's fellowship.

The final state of affairs will be the best of all because as resurrected persons on the new earth, we will have true freedom perfected. Our situation will be even better than that of our first parents because we will not be able to sin. As always, we will have freedom of choice, but as perfected humans beings we will be in a positive relationship with God and will always choose God's glory and never choose to sin.

Indeed, we will serve God in the unhindered true freedom for which we were created.[7]

Free Will and the Reasons Why People Are Saved and Condemned

Some questions have more than one correct answer. If I were asked to describe my religious identity, I could give four correct answers: "I am a Christian, a Protestant, an evangelical, and a Presbyterian." All four are true. I am a Christian, not a Hindu, a Buddhist, or a Muslim. I am a Protestant Christian, not a Roman Catholic or Orthodox Christian. I am an evangelical Christian, not a liberal one. I am a Presbyterian, not an Episcopalian, a Lutheran, or a Baptist. Furthermore, not all of these designations are equally important to me. Being a Christian is more important to me than being a Protestant, which is more important than being an evangelical, which is more important than being a Presbyterian.

Similarly, the Bible gives more than one correct answer to the questions of why people are saved and why they are condemned. In addition, as in the question concerning my religious identity, the various answers to the two questions differ in importance. There are several correct answers, but some are more important than others. Thinking through the reasons why people are saved and lost will help us to better understand the Bible's teaching concerning human free will and its relation to predestination and other sovereign acts of God.

Reasons Why People Are Saved

Scripture gives four good answers to the question: why are people saved? They are saved because the Father chose them before creation, because Christ died and rose to save them,

7. For a pithy summary of human freedom at the different stages of the Bible's story, see chapter 9 of the Westminster Confession of Faith.

because the Holy Spirit opened their hearts, and because they trusted Christ as Savior. Although the four answers differ in degrees of ultimacy, each one is biblical and therefore true. We will treat them in reverse order, beginning with our immediate experience and moving backward in time to eternity.

People Are Saved because They Trust Christ as Lord and Savior. Scripture frequently teaches that human beings are saved from their sins by trusting Christ as Lord and Savior. John writes: "But to all who did receive him [Jesus], who believed in his name, he gave the right to become children of God" (John 1:12). Paul sounds the same note: "If you confess with your mouth that Jesus is Lord and believe in your heart that God raised him from the dead, you will be saved" (Rom. 10:9).

And so does Peter: "Though you do not now see him [Jesus Christ], you believe in him and rejoice with joy that is inexpressible and filled with glory, obtaining the outcome of your faith, the salvation of your souls" (1 Peter 1:8b–9). Examples could easily be multiplied; people come to the Lord by believing that Christ died and rose to deliver them from judgment. This is clear according to Scripture and is not nullified by the fact that there are more ultimate answers to the question why people are saved.

People Are Saved because the Holy Spirit Opens Their Hearts to the Gospel. As we saw when we surveyed free will and the Bible's story, in the fall human beings lost the ability to believe for salvation.[8] As fallen sinners, we are unable to move toward God. Teaching that people must trust Christ to be saved, therefore, is insufficient. We must go beyond that by celebrating the preceding grace of God that enables sinners to believe. Various passages teach that people come to Christ because God enables them to do so.

In his account of Paul's dealings with Lydia in Philippi, Luke underscores that God must work in sinners' lives in order for them to believe. Lydia was among the women gathered by the

8. See pages 128–29.

riverside to pray. When Paul preached, "the Lord opened her heart to pay attention to what was said by" him (Acts 16:14). As a result she believed in Christ, and was baptized along with her family (v. 15). When the Lord opens people's hearts to the gospel, they trust Christ as Lord.

Paul teaches the same thing as he instructs the Corinthians on the proper use of spiritual gifts: "Therefore I want you to understand that . . . no one can say 'Jesus is Lord' except in the Holy Spirit" (1 Cor. 12:3). The Christian confession leading to salvation, as rehearsed in Romans 10:9–10, is that Jesus is Lord. Paul teaches that no one can truly make that confession unless the Spirit works in him or her.

Scripture teaches both that sinners must believe in Christ for salvation and that those in whom the Spirit works will believe. How can we fit these truths together? By maintaining that those in whose lives the Spirit works will trust Christ for eternal life, something they would not have done on their own. God opens people's hearts to Jesus, and by the Spirit they confess that Jesus is Lord (Acts 16:14; 1 Cor. 12:3; see also John 6:44).

People Are Saved because Christ Died and Rose to Save Them. It is important to go further back in history to answer the question why people are saved. People are not saved by believing just anything; according to Scripture, saving faith has specific content. It is faith in one particular person—in him who said: "I am the way, and the truth, and the life. No one comes to the Father except through me" (John 14:6). Of all religious leaders, Jesus Christ alone is the Savior of the world. That this fact is very unpopular in current pluralistic societies, including America's, does not make it any less true. Peter speaks plain words: "And there is salvation in no one else, for there is no other name under heaven given among men by which we must be saved" (Acts 4:12).

Moreover, one is not saved merely by believing historical facts about Jesus—that he was born of the Virgin Mary, performed miracles, died, lived again, ascended to heaven, and will return.

One could believe all those truths and not be saved. Saving faith is faith that Jesus died and was raised to save sinners, as Paul says when he summarizes the gospel: "For I delivered to you as of first importance what I also received: that Christ died for our sins in accordance with the Scriptures, that he was buried, [and] that he was raised on the third day in accordance with the Scriptures" (1 Cor. 15:3–4). People must believe that Jesus died and rose to save them, as Paul told the Philippian jailer: "Believe in the Lord Jesus, and you will be saved, you and your household" (Acts 16:31).

There is thus a third reason why people are saved: "The saying is trustworthy and deserving of full acceptance, that Christ Jesus came into the world to save sinners, of whom I am the foremost" (1 Tim. 1:15). People are saved, then, because they trust Christ, because the Holy Spirit enables them to believe, and because Jesus has loved them and given himself for them. All three are true, although they differ in ultimacy. Most ultimate is the work that Jesus did in the first century. That work establishes our faith; we are saved by believing in Christ's saving work, as the Spirit enables us to believe. But still we have not probed as far as Scripture allows in answering the question of why we are saved.

People Are Saved because the Father Chose Them for Salvation before Creation. The ultimate reason why people are saved is that God the Father chose them for salvation before creation. The Father chose us for final sanctification "before the foundation of the world" (Eph. 1:4). God gave us grace in Christ Jesus "before the ages began" (2 Tim. 1:9). They will fall prey to idolatry whose names have been omitted from the book of life "from the foundation of the world" (Rev. 17:8). Plainly, our salvation does not begin with our faith, or the Spirit's work in our lives, or even Jesus' work in the first century. Ultimately, it begins with God's election of us before creation. The ultimate reason why people are saved is that God loved and chose them before he created the heavens and the earth.

An Attempt to Relate the Four Reasons Why People Are Saved.
Understanding the biblical relations between the four reasons
why people are saved increases our understanding of our free will
and God's free grace. First, note that all four reasons are biblical.
It is God's truth that believers in Christ will be saved, that the Holy
Spirit opens people to the gospel, that Christ's death and resurrection are the only cure for the disease of sin, and that God elected
his people for salvation before creation.

Second, the four reasons are not equally ultimate, but they
progressively reach further back in history until before creation.
Although it is true that we believed unto salvation, the Spirit's
work in us is more ultimate because without his work we would
not have believed. And Christ's work in the first century is more
ultimate still because without it we would have nothing to believe
to be saved and the Spirit would have no saving work to apply.
Finally, of course, God's planning is most ultimate because it took
place before creation.

Third, although we cannot perfectly explain how it is so, the
more ultimate reasons for salvation do not undermine the less
ultimate ones. The fact that God chose does not nullify the work
of Christ, but establishes it, for Christ came to do the Father's will
(John 6:38–40; 17:2, 6, 9, 24; Heb. 10:7). The facts that God chose
and Christ redeems do not nullify the Spirit's work in hearts, but
rather establish it, for the Spirit applies the salvation planned by
the Father and accomplished by the Son. Most importantly for
this chapter, the Father's election, the Son's redemption, and the
Spirit's working in hearts do not diminish our faith but establish
it. It is those whom God chose who believe (John 6:37; Acts 13:48;
Rom. 8:29–30; 9:22–24). The work of Christ is the content of our
faith. And the Spirit enables those to believe who never would have
done so without his aid (John 6:44, 65; 1 Cor. 2:14; 2 Cor. 4:4).

Reasons Why People Are Condemned

There are also multiple answers to the question of why persons are condemned: because of their actual sins, because of

Adam's original sin, and because of God's passing over them (reprobation).

People Are Condemned because of Their Actual Sins. Both Testaments affirm that God will condemn sinners because they misused their free will.

> As the LORD of hosts purposed to deal with us for our ways and deeds, so has he dealt with us. (Zech. 1:6b; see also Hos. 4:9)

> Do not marvel at this, for an hour is coming when all who are in the tombs will hear his voice and come out, those who have done good to the resurrection of life, and those who have done evil to the resurrection of judgment. (John 5:28–29)

> But for those who are self-seeking and do not obey the truth, but obey unrighteousness, there will be wrath and fury. There will be tribulation and distress for every human being who does evil, the Jew first and also the Greek. (Rom. 2:8–9; see also Gal. 6:7–8)

It is not difficult to discern a consistent pattern: many passages teach that a holy and just God will give sinners what they deserve. Judgment is according to deeds—or, more exactly, according to thoughts (1 Cor. 4:5), words (Matt. 12:36), and deeds (Rev. 20:12–13). And people who all their lives sow evil thoughts, words, and deeds will reap God's wrath. When one asks why sinners are condemned, Scripture's predominant answer is obvious: the abuse of human free will to commit sins.

People Are Condemned because of Adam's Original Sin. The Bible also teaches that people perish because of the original sin of Adam, our representative in the garden of Eden. Paul asserts this truth in Romans 5:

> Many died through one man's trespass. . . .

138

For the judgment following one trespass brought condemnation. . . .

Because of one man's trespass, death reigned through that one man. . . .

Therefore, . . . one trespass led to condemnation for all men. . . .

For . . . by the one man's disobedience the many were made sinners. . . . (Rom. 5:15, 16, 17, 18, 19)

When emphasizing human freedom, Scripture reveals that people are lost because of both original sin and actual sins. Original sin is obviously more ultimate than actual sins because it was committed by the first man. And it is the reason why actual sins occur; when Adam fell, "sin came into the world through one man" (Rom. 5:12). But note that Scripture does not regard original sin as nullifying sinners' responsibility for their actual sins. This is proved by the fact that before Romans treats original sin (in 5:12–19), it has much to say about actual sins (in 1:18–3:20). Original sin is more ultimate than actual sin, but both are genuine reasons why people are condemned.

People Are Condemned because God Passed over Them (Reprobation). Although the accent of the judgment passages is on sinners' abuse of freedom, a few passages teach that God is sovereign over the destiny of the lost. Overwhelmingly, the gospel of John points to people's evil and unbelief as the reasons for their condemnation (e.g., John 3:18–20; 5:28–29). But a few times it reveals that God is in charge of the fate of the lost. In his Good Shepherd Discourse, Jesus utters startling words:

I did tell you, but you do not believe. The miracles I do in my Father's name speak for me, but you do not believe because you are not my sheep. My sheep listen to my voice; I know them, and they follow me. I give them eternal life, and they shall never perish." (John 10:25–28 NIV)

First, Jesus charges the Jewish leaders with unbelief. His words and works leave them without excuse for rejecting him. Then Jesus says the opposite of what we might expect. He does not say, "You are not my sheep because you do not believe." Rather, he says, "You do not believe because you are not my sheep." One of John's election themes is the prior identity of those who are God's people and of those who are not. God's people, having been chosen by God, favorably respond to Jesus' messages and miracles. Others, who are not God's people, reject the Son of God. We will call the two groups sheep and goats, respectively.

Jesus says that the sheep hear his voice (believe on him), that he knows them (savingly), and that they follow him. But he tells the goats, "You do not believe because you are not my sheep" (John 10:26 NIV). These are strong words indeed. People are goats before they respond to Jesus, and they reject him because they are goats. This is reprobation—God's passing over those whom he allows to pay the penalty for their own sins.[9]

Peter also affirms that God is Lord over the destiny of the wicked. He teaches that Jesus the Messiah is "a living stone rejected by men but in the sight of God chosen and precious" (1 Peter 2:4). He then contrasts the fates of the righteous and the wicked:

> So the honor is for you who believe, but for those who do not believe, "The stone that the builders rejected has become the cornerstone," and "A stone of stumbling, and a rock of offense." They stumble because they disobey the word, as they were destined to do. (1 Peter 2:7–8, quoting Ps. 118:22; Isa. 8:14)

Believers are honored, but unbelievers stumble over the most important stone of all. Peter's words are severe: "They stumble because they disobey the word, as they were destined to do" (1 Peter 2:8b). Sometimes Peter uses "obedience" as synonymous with "faith" (1:2, 22) and "do not obey" or "disobey" as synony-

9. The technical term for God's passing them by is "preterition"; see Louis Berkhof, *Systematic Theology* (Grand Rapids: Eerdmans, 1939, 1941), 116.

mous with "disbelieve" (2:8; 3:1, 20; 4:17). When, therefore, he says that unbelievers "disobey the word," he means that they do not believe the word of salvation, the gospel. He explains, "They disobey the word, as they were destined to do." Here again Scripture teaches that God destines the fate of unbelievers. Although they are condemned because they "do not obey the gospel of God" (4:17), God is nonetheless Lord of their destiny.

The greatest last-judgment passage appears in Revelation 20:11–15. This text is notable because it presents the fates of human beings in terms of both divine sovereignty and human freedom. The major accent is on human culpability: God damns the unsaved for their evil deeds. The dead are judged according to their deeds, as those deeds were recorded in God's books of judgment (Rev. 20:12–13).

The passage also tells of the opening of another book at the last judgment—the book of life. "The book of life" (Rev. 3:5; 17:8; 20:12, 15) or "the Lamb's book of life" (21:27; see also 13:8) is frequently mentioned in Revelation. Since only the ones whose names are recorded in "the Lamb's book of life" will enter the New Jerusalem (21:27), the book serves as the census register of the city of God. Moreover, the names of the saints have been enrolled "in the book of life *from the foundation of the world*" (17:8).

When John says, therefore, "If anyone's name was not found written in the book of life, he was thrown into the lake of fire" (Rev. 20:15), he speaks of God's sovereignty over the destiny of the lost. To have one's name recorded in the book of life from creation is to belong to the people of God. Not to have one's name written in the book of life is to be rejected by God in reprobation. God enrolls people in the book of life by his mysterious election; he chooses who will be registered in the New Jerusalem.

When John tells of the books that have recorded people's deeds and of the book of life, then, he speaks of human freedom and God's sovereignty, respectively. Both free will and sovereignty are true. Sinners get what they deserve from the hand of a just God at the last judgment. But at the same time God stands behind the fate of every person, including the unsaved.

An Attempt to Relate the Three Reasons Why People Are Condemned. We must strive for a scriptural sense of proper proportion when relating the three reasons why people are condemned. The order, from least to greatest ultimacy, is: actual sin, original sin, and reprobation. It is vital to understand that the Bible gives these three reasons why people perish and does not regard any one of them as canceling out the others. To be faithful to Scripture, we must do the same. It is foolish to exalt our reason unduly and harmonize matters that the Scriptures leave in tension, because such harmony comes with a price—distortion of the Bible's witness.

A Summary of Why People Are Saved and Condemned

In order to properly understand free will, we must heed biblical teaching concerning why people are saved and lost. God is the sovereign Judge before whom all sinners will stand on judgment day. Scripture teaches that people will be condemned for three reasons—chiefly because they have abused their freedom in rebellion against their Creator. But there is more to the story. Behind all actual sins is Adam's original sin. It is the way the Bible accounts for the existence of sin in God's good world. But original sin in no way nullifies the truth that sinners deserve God's condemnation for their own sins. If we probe as far as Scripture allows concerning eternal destinies, we learn that before creation, God in grace chose multitudes for salvation in predestination and passed over others in reprobation, permitting them to pay the penalty for their sins.

With Scripture we affirm that God is Lord over the destiny of every human being. But with Scripture we also affirm that his lordship is asymmetrical with respect to the saved and the lost. He is proactive in election: he gives grace to those who would otherwise perish. He is passive in reprobation, planning to allow sinners to reap what they have sown. Here again we must underscore a key point: God's reprobation does not cancel either original sin or actual sin. Although we cannot explain how this

is so, we affirm its truth, even as we affirm the mysteries of the
Trinity and of Christ's two natures.

In sum: sinners have freedom of choice, but in the fall lost
true freedom. As a result, they are unable to believe the gospel
on their own and need the Spirit's help. So it is a mistake to
exaggerate the free will that human beings possess since the
fall. The elect truly believe, but only because the Spirit overcomes their slavery to sin, liberates their will, and enables them
to believe. Although sinners lack the ability even to believe,
God holds them responsible and will condemn them for their
actual sins.

Admittedly, we do not have all the answers. For example,
how can God pass over human beings and still hold them responsible for their sins? A part of our difficulty in understanding is
due to the mystery of divine sovereignty and human responsibility, a topic that forms our third perspective on the freedom
of the will.

Free Will and Its Relation to God's Sovereignty

The Bible Affirms Both Divine Sovereignty and Genuine Human Responsibility

A third viewpoint that helps us understand free will is its
relation to God's sovereign control of all things. Scripture affirms
divine sovereignty, and at the same time teaches that there is
human freedom in the sense of genuine human responsibility
to God. We can understand much of the relation between them,
but mystery remains.

The Bible Affirms Divine Sovereignty. Both Testaments testify to God's absolute sway over all his creatures and all their
actions.

> The LORD brings the counsel of the nations to nothing;
> he frustrates the plans of the peoples.

The counsel of the LORD stands forever,
    the plans of his heart to all generations. (Ps. 33:10–11)

The LORD has established his throne in the heavens,
    and his kingdom rules over all. (Ps. 103:19)

Your eyes saw my unformed substance;
in your book were written, every one of them,
    the days that were formed for me,
    when as yet there were none of them. (Ps. 139:16)

This is the purpose that is purposed
    concerning the whole earth,
and this is the hand that is stretched out
    over all the nations.
For the LORD of hosts has purposed,
    and who will annul it?
His hand is stretched out,
    and who will turn it back? (Isa. 14:26–27)

For from him and through him and to him are all things. To
him be glory forever. Amen. (Rom. 11:36)

In him we have obtained an inheritance, having been predestined according to the purpose of him who works all things
according to the counsel of his will. (Eph. 1:11)

The Lord God Almighty, the Maker of the heavens and
the earth, rules over all nations (Ps. 33:10–11; Isa. 14:26–27),
individuals (Ps. 139:16), and generations (Ps. 33:10–11)—in
fact, "over all" (Ps. 103:19; see also Eph. 1:11). No one can
thwart God's plans (Ps. 33:10–11; Isa. 14:26–27). He is Creator,
Sustainer, and Consummator of all (Rom. 11:36). In short, he
is the sovereign Lord.

The Bible Affirms Genuine Human Responsibility. Both Testaments also testify to the reality of our accountability to God.

144

In fact, it is as easy to find verses teaching human responsibility as it is to find those teaching divine control.

> Then the LORD said to Moses, "Behold, I am about to rain bread from heaven for you, and the people shall go out and gather a day's portion every day, that I may test them, whether they will walk in my law or not." (Ex. 16:4)

> And if it is evil in your eyes to serve the LORD, choose this day whom you will serve, whether the gods your fathers served in the region beyond the River, or the gods of the Amorites in whose land you dwell. But as for me and my house, we will serve the LORD. (Josh. 24:15)

> Everyone who is arrogant in heart is an abomination to
> the LORD;
> be assured, he will not go unpunished. (Prov. 16:5)

> The soul who sins shall die. The son shall not suffer for the iniquity of the father, nor the father suffer for the iniquity of the son. The righteousness of the righteous shall be upon himself, and the wickedness of the wicked shall be upon himself. . . .
> Cast away from you all the transgressions that you have committed, and make yourselves a new heart and a new spirit! Why will you die, O house of Israel? For I have no pleasure in the death of anyone, declares the Lord GOD; so turn, and live. (Ezek. 18:20, 31–32)

> For God did not send his Son into the world to condemn the world, but in order that the world might be saved through him. Whoever believes in him is not condemned, but whoever does not believe is condemned already, because he has not believed in the name of the only Son of God. (John 3:17–18)

> But whoever has doubts is condemned if he eats, because the eating is not from faith. For whatever does not proceed from faith is sin. (Rom. 14:23)

To the weak I became weak, that I might win the weak. I have become all things to all people, that by all means I might save some. (1 Cor. 9:22)

As he who called you is holy, you also be holy in all your conduct, since it is written, "You shall be holy, for I am holy." (1 Peter 1:15–16)

God created human beings responsible to him. It matters whether or not we believe in Christ (John 3:17–18), worship the Lord (Josh. 24:15), obey God (Ex. 16:4; Ezek. 18:20), and evangelize (1 Cor. 9:22). He holds us accountable for our actions, requiring us to worship him only (Josh. 24:15), to act in faith (Rom. 14:23), and to be holy as he is holy (1 Peter 1:15–16). He tests his people (Ex. 16:4) and punishes their sin and disobedience (Prov. 16:5; Ezek. 18:20, 31–32).

The Bible Affirms Divine Sovereignty and Human Responsibility Together. Scripture not only teaches both absolute divine control and real human responsibility, but often does so in the same passage! In the quotations below, references to God's sovereignty are underlined and references to human responsibility are in italics. Note the interplay between the two.

And now do not be distressed or angry with yourselves because you sold me here, for God sent me before you to preserve life. . . . So it was not you who sent me here, but God. He has made me . . . ruler over all the land of Egypt. (Gen. 45:5, 8)

As for you, you meant evil against me, but God meant it for good, to bring it about that many people should be kept alive, as they are today. (Gen. 50:20)

Consecrate yourselves, therefore, and be holy, for I am the LORD your God. *Keep my statutes and do them;* I am the LORD who sanctifies you. (Lev. 20:7–8)

146

Ah, Assyria, the rod of my anger . . . ! Against a godless nation I send him, and against the people of my wrath I command him, to take spoil and seize plunder. . . . *But he does not so intend, and his heart does not so think; but it is in his heart to destroy, and to cut off nations not a few.* . . . Shall the axe boast over him who hews with it, or the saw magnify itself against him who wields it? As if a rod should wield him who lifts it, or as if a staff should lift him who is not wood! Therefore the Lord GOD of hosts will send wasting sickness among his stout warriors." (Isa. 10:5–7, 15–16)

For the Son of Man goes as it has been determined, *but woe to that man by whom he is betrayed!* (Luke 22:22)

This Jesus, delivered up according to the definite plan and foreknowledge of God, *you crucified and killed by the hands of lawless men.* (Acts 2:23)

For truly in this city there were gathered together against your holy servant Jesus, whom you anointed, both Herod and Pontius Pilate, along with the Gentiles and the peoples of Israel, to do whatever your hand and your plan had predestined to take place. (Acts 4:27–28)

And the Lord said to Paul one night in a vision, *"Do not be afraid, but go on speaking and do not be silent,* for I am with you, and no one will attack you to harm you, for I have many in this city who are my people." (Acts 18:9–10)

Therefore, my beloved, as you have always obeyed, so now, not only as in my presence but much more in my absence, *work out your own salvation with fear and trembling,* for it is God who works in you, both to will and to work for his good pleasure. (Phil. 2:12–13)

Joseph's brothers sin grievously against him by selling him into slavery, but God overrules and brings much good out of their sin, including the family's deliverance (Gen. 45:5,

8; 50:20). The wicked nation of Assyria devastates the northern kingdom of Israel, but without Assyria knowing that it is a tool in the hand of Israel's God (Isa. 10:5–7, 15–16). And God punishes wicked Assyria for its subsequent boasting against him (Isa. 10:15–16).

The Lord both commands Israel to be holy and declares that he is the sanctifier (Lev. 20:7–8). Jesus both announces that God ordained his betrayal and condemns his betrayer (Luke 22:22). Jesus' crucifixion is both a terrible crime and a preordained act of God (Acts 2:23; 4:27–28). God both commands Paul to keep preaching in Corinth and assures him of divine protection and successful ministry (Acts 18:9–10). Paul both commands the Philippians to live in the fear of the Lord and assures them that God works in them to bring about his will (Phil. 2:12–13).

Parameters for Sovereignty and Responsibility

Fatalism Must Be Rejected as an Error. Critics sometimes unfairly lump together the Calvinist view of divine sovereignty with fatalism. But what is the difference? The former is a biblical view and the latter a pagan one. According to Scripture, God is a person who is holy, just, good, faithful, loving, all-wise, powerful, and more. Furthermore, this great God enters into covenant with his people and promises to be their God, to take them for his people, to bring them to know him, and to forgive their sins (Gen. 17:7; Jer. 31:33–34; Matt. 26:28).

Donald Bloesch provides the following description of classical Greek fatalism:

> Fate, personified by the Greeks under the name of Moira, signified in the ancient world the unseen power that rules over human destiny. . . . Fate is . . . a cosmic determinism that has no ultimate meaning or purpose. . . . Fate is blind, inscrutable, and inescapable.
>
> Fate means the abrogation of human freedom. . . . Fate is the rule of contingency that casts a pall over all human striving.

148

Fate makes the future precarious and uncertain. . . . Fate is impersonal and irrational. . . .

Fatalism was present among the ancient Stoics, and it pervades much of the thought of Hinduism, Buddhism, and Islam.[10]

In contrast with the personal God of Scripture, fatalism says that human beings and the world are ruled by impersonal forces. Over against the Bible's idea of God's covenant with his people, fatalism teaches "que sera sera": "whatever will be, will be." In contrast with God's pledging to be faithful to his people (Gen. 15:1, 7, 9–11, 17), fatalism denies certainty because people are at the whim of fate. Against the biblical teaching that God treats his people as responsible covenant partners, fatalism denies that human actions have any effect on history.

Absolute Power to Contrary Must Be Rejected as an Error. If fatalism must be rejected as an incorrect view of God's sovereignty, what philosophers call "absolute power to contrary" must also be rejected as an incorrect view of human responsibility. Absolute power to contrary, or the power of contrary choice, is the view that creatures can ultimately frustrate the will of their Creator. Although God holds human beings responsible for their actions, they cannot finally defeat God's plan and will:

No wisdom, no understanding, no counsel can avail against the LORD. (Prov. 21:30)

I am God, and there is no other . . . , declaring the end from the beginning . . . , saying, "My counsel shall stand, and I will accomplish all my purpose." . . . I have spoken, and I will bring it to pass; I have purposed, and I will do it. (Isa. 46:9–11)

To affirm absolute power to contrary is to make God dependent on human beings. God is dependent on his people in the

10. D. G. Bloesch, "Fate, Fatalism," in Walter A. Elwell, ed., *Evangelical Dictionary of Theology*, 2nd ed. (Grand Rapids: Baker, 2001), 439.

sense that he makes a covenant with them and responds to their praise, obedience, and prayers. But he is not absolutely dependent on people, for he is God and they are his creatures.

> All the inhabitants of the earth are accounted as nothing, and he does according to his will . . . among the inhabitants of the earth; and none can stay his hand or say to him, "What have you done?" (Dan. 4:35)

> In him we have obtained an inheritance, having been predestined according to the purpose of him who works all things according to the counsel of his will. (Eph. 1:11)

Setting Parameters. So far, we have affirmed absolute divine control and real human responsibility, and rejected the errors of fatalism and absolute power to contrary. Figure 1 summarizes our findings.[11]

Figure 1: Parameters for sovereignty and responsibility.

In this diagram, "DS" stands for acts of divine sovereignty and "HR" for acts of human responsibility. In rejecting the errors of fatalism and absolute power to contrary, we have set parameters beside the sovereignty of God and human responsibility, respectively. The fact that some acts have only "DS" written for them indicates that certain deeds are performed by God alone, such as creating the world and raising the dead.

Notice, however, that many deeds are performed by both God and human beings at the same time. The brothers of Joseph

11. I am indebted to D. A. Carson's *Divine Sovereignty and Human Responsibility: Biblical Perspectives in Tension* (Grand Rapids: Baker, 1994) for guidance on relating sovereignty and human responsibility.

sell him into slavery, intending to harm him, but God brings Joseph to Egypt and overrides his brothers' evil intentions for good (Gen. 45:8; 50:20). Wicked human beings crucify the Son of God, but God causes the wrath of men to praise him and uses the death of Christ to accomplish eternal redemption (Acts 2:23; 4:27–28).

This is the principle of double agency: at the same time, certain acts are the acts of God and human beings. Joseph's words to his brothers reveal an important truth: "You meant evil against me, but God meant it for good" (Gen. 50:20). The early Christians prayed to God, acknowledging that wicked Jews and Gentiles had conspired to kill Jesus, but in so doing managed only "to do whatever your hand and your plan had predestined to take place" (Acts 4:28).

Reflecting on the passages that teach double agency can rescue us from wrong thinking. Although text after text shows that God is absolutely sovereign, not once is he portrayed as the author of sin. God is never to be charged with evil. And although God is in control of all things, including evil, sinful acts do not for that reason become righteous ones. Instead, they remain sins and odious in the sight of a holy God. Judas, Caiaphas, Herod, and Pilate are not heroes in the biblical story but villains.

Reflection protects us from another error. Though God is Lord of all, we are not pawns or puppets. We are genuinely accountable to God. Joseph's brothers were not coerced by God to sell him into slavery. Of their own volition they declared: "Here comes this dreamer. Come now, let us kill him and throw him into one of the pits" (Gen. 37:19–20). As human beings we have genuine responsibility. It makes a difference whether or not we believe in Jesus, pray, or evangelize, to cite three examples.

Coming face to face with double agency humbles us. We cannot fully explain how it works. This in turn teaches us an important lesson: it is not good for us to imagine that we understand more of God and his ways than we really do. We understand in part, but we also do not understand in part. The mystery of dual agency remains. It is good for us to be humbled before the great God of the Bible, creation, providence, and redemption. It is very good indeed, for it puts us in our place under the mighty hand of God.

To Emphasize Either Sovereignty or Responsibility at the Expense of the Other Is to Fall into the Error of Rationalism

Two opposite extremes must be avoided: hyper-Calvinism and Arminianism. Ironically, although they are polar opposites, at root they are the same type of error. They both end up exalting human reason over a large portion of the Bible's witness.

Hyper-Calvinism Is an Error. Hyper-Calvinism makes a good start because it begins with scores of biblical passages, including the ones we quoted above, that affirm God's absolute control over whatever comes to pass. But hyper-Calvinists, being unwilling to give adequate weight to an equally impressive number of Scriptures that teach genuine human responsibility, minimize human responsibility or deny it outright. Hyper-Calvinists have taught that God does not answer prayer; rather, we pray for our own benefit. While benefit comes to those who pray, the Bible plainly teaches that God answers prayer (see, e.g., Matt. 7:7–11). Hyper-Calvinism has also downplayed or opposed evangelism in the name of God's sovereign grace. Scripture teaches God's sovereign grace, and it also teaches that the sovereign Lord of all has ordained the use of evangelism as the means of bringing his people to himself (Matt. 28:19–20). In the end, in spite of its good beginning, hyper-Calvinism is a form of rationalism—elevating human reason above some of the truths of God's Word.

Arminianism Is an Error. One of the great ironies of the history of Christian theology is that Arminianism, the archen-

152

emy of hyper-Calvinism, is also a form of rationalism. Arminianism, too, starts off well, pointing to an abundance of biblical evidence for human responsibility, including the verses we quoted above. But in refusing to accept the Bible's testimony to God's absolute sovereignty, it redefines God's sovereignty in terms of its understanding of free will. As a result, according to Arminianism, God sovereignly relinquishes some of his control out of respect for human freedom. Consequently, his predestination is reduced to his foreseeing people's response to the gospel and ratifying foreseen human decision. But we have seen over and over again in these pages that God's predestination is not based "on human will or exertion, but on God, who has mercy" (Rom. 9:16). Whereas Arminianism insists that the ultimate factors in salvation are human faith and perseverance foreseen by God, Scripture teaches that the ultimate factors are God's "love . . . according to the purpose of his will" (Eph. 1:4–5), "his own purpose and grace" (2 Tim. 1:9).

Ironically, although hyper-Calvinism and Arminianism are opposite ways of viewing salvation, the first overemphasizing God's control, the second overemphasizing human freedom, in the end they are both forms of rationalism. They both start with large quantities of God's truth, but both depreciate other equally biblical truths by making human reason the arbiter in theology.

Conclusion

Only by viewing free will in relation to God's sovereignty can we understand it aright. Scripture affirms both absolute divine sovereignty and genuine responsibility; in fact, it puts them together in many passages. God thus invites us to hold his sovereignty and our accountability in tension. We affirm them both and sharpen our understanding by rejecting fatalism and absolute power to contrary because both conflict with the Bible's presentation of God and his people in covenant. The mystery of double agency remains; many events in Scripture are regarded as the actions of God and of human beings. Therefore, the best solution is to admit that we do not have the perfect solution. In fact, to "solve" the problem of the dynamic biblical interplay between God's absolute control and real but limited human responsibility is to fall into rationalism, as hyper-Calvinism and Arminianism bear out.

The Bible's Story of Election

- Act One: The Old Testament
  - Scene One: The Election of Abraham and of Jacob (Israel)
  - Scene Two: The Election of the Nation of Israel
- Act Two: The New Testament
  - Scene One: The Election of the Messiah
  - Scene Two: The Election of the Twelve Disciples

Act One: The Old Testament

Scene One: The Election of Abraham and of Jacob (Israel)

The story of election begins in the Old Testament, where God enters into covenant with one man and thereby ultimately brings salvation to the world. That man is Abraham, and God's choice of him is an amazing example of election. Despite the fact that Abraham hails from an idolatrous family (Josh. 24:2–3), God calls him to leave Ur, promising to bless him and, through him, to bless the world (Gen. 12:1–3). God swears to him, "I will establish my covenant between me and you and your offspring after you throughout their generations for an everlasting covenant, to be God to you and to your offspring after you" (Gen. 17:7). God gives Abraham and Sarah, his wife, a barren couple, a child to whom God extends his promises made to Abraham—Isaac.

155

The Lord causes Isaac's wife, Rebekah, to become pregnant with twins, Esau and Jacob. Although Jacob is an unethical man (Gen. 27:19, 24, 35; 31:20, 31), God has chosen him before birth to display his "purpose in election" (Rom. 9:11) and to further his promises to Abraham. God promises to bring a nation from Jacob (Gen. 25:23; Mal. 1:2–3). God accomplishes this by changing Jacob's name to "Israel," by giving him twelve sons, each of whom would father a tribe, and by uniting the tribes in a nation—the nation of Israel.

Scene Two: The Election of the Nation of Israel

The Old Testament story of election begins with Abraham and Jacob (Israel), but it concentrates on God's election of the nation of Israel. God tells Israel, "It was not because you were more in number than any other people that the LORD set his love on you and chose you, for you were the fewest of all peoples" (Deut. 7:7). Israel's election is based on God's love (Deut. 4:37; 10:15), not because of any goodness he sees in it, for the Old Testament consistently presents Israel as a rebellious people.

God's choice of Israel is particular. He does not choose Egypt, Assyria, or Babylon, but chooses Israel alone out of all the nations (Deut. 7:6; 10:15; 14:2). Although some might think this is unfair, it is God's gracious act to one sinful people among all that deserved his judgment.

Although God owns everything, he still loves and chooses Israel to be his own people, his peculiar treasure (Deut. 7:6; 14:2). He imparts grace upon grace when he delivers the chosen nation from Egyptian bondage (Deut. 4:37; 7:6). Furthermore, God's election brings great responsibility to the covenant people. Because of God's choice, Israel is to live as a holy nation, to fear the Lord, and to love aliens (Deut. 7:1–6; 10:19–20; 14:1–2).

It is at the point of Israel's covenant responsibility that our story turns sour. In spite of God's lavishing his grace on Israel, the nation repeatedly breaks covenant with its Lord and incurs his judgment. Israel's covenant Lord sends the nation into captivity, first the northern kingdom in 722 BC, and then the southern kingdom in 586 BC. Although God restores the nation after seventy years of captivity, it has still not learned its lesson. The last book of the Old Testament tells of Israel's ongoing rebellion against the Lord (Mal. 1:6–8; 2:10–11, 13–14; 3:7–9, 13–15) and mentions only a faithful remnant (Mal. 3:16–18).

Were it not for God's grace, the story of election would have ended here. But because God is compassionate and faithful to his promises to Abraham, Isaac, and Jacob, he still intends to bless "all the families of the earth" through them (Gen. 12:3). But it would not be through the unfaithful nation of Israel. Rather, as Isaiah had prophesied (Isa. 42:1), God would send his chosen servant to do for the nation (and more!) what the nation had failed to do. Act Two puts the spotlight on this chosen Israelite, the Messiah, the Lord Jesus.

Act Two: The New Testament

The change from Act One to Act Two is brought about by the progression of the Bible's story from the Old Testament to the New, which in turn is brought about by the coming of Jesus the Christ, the Mediator of the new covenant.

Scene One: The Election of the Messiah

Jesus' Election. A minor Old Testament theme, with far-reaching consequences, is Isaiah's teaching that the Messiah is chosen by God: "Behold my servant, whom I uphold, *my chosen*, in whom my soul delights; I have put my Spirit upon him; he will bring forth justice to the nations" (Isa. 42:1). Although when Isaiah writes of the servant of the Lord he sometimes refers to Israel, here he predicts the coming of the Messiah (Christ) to accomplish a mission. These words are fulfilled in Jesus' person and ministry.

Matthew records that after Jesus healed a man who had a withered hand, the Pharisees conspired to destroy Jesus (Matt. 12:9–14). Aware of this, he withdrew, many of the people followed him, and he healed many more. When Jesus ordered his followers not to publicize his ministry (v. 16), he fulfilled Isaiah's prediction, "He will not quarrel or cry aloud . . . ; a bruised reed he will not break, and a smoldering wick he will not quench" (Matt. 12:19–20, quoting Isa. 42:2–3). Matthew thereby identifies Jesus with the one whom the Lord calls "my servant whom I have chosen" (Matt. 12:18, quoting Isa. 42:1). Thus, not only are Abraham, Isaac, and the nation of Israel chosen, but Christ is also chosen. Why is this?

Luke answers this question in two places where he indicates that Jesus is chosen of God. At Jesus' transfiguration on a mountain, where he was praying with Peter, James, and John, Moses and Elijah appeared in glory (Luke 9:28–31). Foolishly, Peter proposed to make three tents, one each for Jesus, Moses, and Elijah. Then a cloud of God's presence overshadowed them, and the Father proclaimed: "This is my Son, my Chosen One; listen to him!" (v. 35; cf. Deut. 18:15). In thus proclaiming, the Father indicated that as the Chosen One, Jesus had been sent into the world to be a prophet. He had also been chosen and sent to be our Redeemer. That role is hinted at by what Moses and Elijah discuss with Jesus—"his departure, which he was about to accomplish at Jerusalem" (v. 31). The word "departure" is *exodus* in Greek, which corresponds as a type to the great Old Testament event of redemption. Jesus' death is the New Testament *exodus* that will redeem all who trust him.

Luke alone reports the Jewish rulers' mocking of Jesus on the cross: "He saved others; let him save himself, if he is the Christ of God, his Chosen One!" (Luke 23:35). Unintentionally, they speak for God when they ridicule the crucified Jesus as God's "Chosen One." He was! As the divine-human Redeemer, he was chosen to die on the cross for sinners.

Peter also teaches that Jesus was chosen by God for a redemption mission. He speaks of "the precious blood of Christ, . . . foreknown before the foundation of the world . . . , a living stone rejected by men but in the sight of God *chosen* and precious" (1 Peter 1:19–20; 2:4).

Jesus' Mission. It is critical to see that Jesus' election pertains to his mission. The Father chose the incarnate Son to be the Lord's servant prophesied in Isaiah 42:1 (Matt. 12:18). He chose him as the God-*man* to be Prophet (Luke 9:31) and Redeemer (Luke 9:31; 23:35). Christ's election has to do with his becoming one of us to redeem us. But how does his election compare with ours? His is like ours in that he and we were chosen by God as human beings. But Christ's election is unlike ours in that we were chosen as sinful human beings for salvation but he as the divine-sinless human to be our Savior.

As the Chosen One, Jesus supplants the nation of Israel. The first words of the New Testament herald Jesus as the true Israelite: "The book of the genealogy of Jesus Christ, the son of David, the son of Abraham" (Matt. 1:1). He is of David's royal line and Abraham's seed. And Matthew's gospel continues to present him as the One who takes Israel's place. After Jesus' birth, an angel warns Joseph to take his family to Egypt to escape Herod's wrath. "This was to fulfill what the Lord had spoken by the prophet, 'Out of Egypt I called my son'" (Matt. 2:15b, quoting Hos. 11:1). What Hosea said concerning Israel is applied by Matthew to the Christ because Israel is a type of the One who takes the place of the nation.

Like Israel, Jesus returns from Egypt (Matt. 2:19–21). Like Israel, tested for forty years in the desert, Jesus fasted for forty days in the wilderness before his temptation (Matt. 4:1–11). Like Israel, which passed through the waters of the Red Sea, so Christ encountered the water of baptism (Matt. 3:16–17). Like Moses, who delivered God's Ten Commandments from Mount Sinai, Jesus, the new lawgiver, preached the Sermon on the Mount (Matt. 5–7). By drawing parallels between Old Testament Israel and Jesus the Messiah, Matthew shows that the true Israelite has come, he who succeeds where the nation failed.

John's gospel shouts that Jesus is the true Israel. He is the Lamb of God, who renders obsolete all Old Testament sacrifices (John 1:29). His body, not the temple, is the ultimate dwelling place of God (2:14–22). He is the true Manna that came from heaven (6:32–35, 57–58). Israel failed to be a light to the nations, but Jesus is the Light of the World (9:5). He existed before Abraham, who anticipated Jesus' coming (8:56–58). In place of Israel's unfaithful shepherds, Jesus is the Good Shepherd who dies for his sheep (10:11, 15). He is the true Vine, replacing Israel, the unfruitful vine of the Lord (15:1–11, 16). John presents overwhelming evidence that Jesus is the true Israelite, who supersedes the failed nation.

According to the writer to the Hebrews, Jesus the Son of God is superior to Old Testament prophets (Heb. 1:1–2), angels (1:3–14), Moses (3:3–6), and the high priests, including Aaron (5:1–6; 7:11–28). Therefore, Christ's offering of himself once for all time supplants the whole Old Testament sacrificial system, as Hebrews repeatedly declares:

> The former priests were many in number, because they were prevented by death from continuing in office, but he holds his priesthood permanently, because he continues forever. (Heb. 7:23–24; see also 7:11)

> In speaking of a new covenant, he makes the first one obsolete. And what is becoming obsolete and growing old is ready to vanish away. (8:13; see also 8:6)

> And every priest stands daily at his service, offering repeatedly the same sacrifices, which can never take away sins. But when Christ had offered for all time a single sacrifice for sins, he sat down at the right hand of God. (10:11–12; see also 9:25–26)

Christ annuls the Mosaic covenant and fulfills the Abrahamic covenant. He is the perfect Israelite, the Mediator of the new covenant, and Savior of the world. He so fulfills and supersedes Judaism that Jews who profess him and later return to Judaism commit spiritual suicide (Heb. 2:2–3; 3:12–14; 6:4–6; 10:26–31; 12:25–29).

Jesus' Teaching. Arminian New Testament scholar Grant Osborne correctly says, "The election motif is an important element in the theology of Jesus."[1] This is evident in a number of places in the New Testament.

1. In the Synoptic Gospels. The election of Old Testament Israel was a historical election, including both saved and unsaved Israelites. By contrast, "the elect" individuals of whom Jesus speaks are chosen for salvation because at his return, he will gather them to share in his kingdom (Mark 13:20, 22, 27). Jesus' teaching on election here (also unlike that of Old Testament Israel) includes Gentiles because he says that the gospel must first be preached to all the nations (v. 10) before the elect will be gathered "from the four winds, from the ends of the earth to the ends of heaven" (v. 27).

2. In the gospel of John. Jesus also teaches about election in the fourth gospel, using the pictures of the Father's giving of people to him for salvation and of people's belonging to him before they believe in him. When Jesus says, "All that the Father gives me will come to me" (John 6:37), he teaches that predestination precedes faith and results in faith.

Jesus teaches God's prior election or rejection of people for salvation. He does this when he divides his hearers into either sheep or nonsheep (goats) and says that they are either sheep or goats *before* they respond to him (John 10:26–30). Their response of faith or unbelief does not *make* them either sheep or goats, but *shows* their prior identities.

Jesus is portrayed as choosing people for salvation only in John 15:14–19. He warns the disciples: "If you were of the world, the world would love you as its own; but because you are not of the world, but I chose you out of the world, therefore the world hates you" (v. 19). Jesus' choice of the eleven disciples "out of

1. Grant Osborne, "Exegetical Notes on Calvinist Texts," in *Grace Unlimited*, ed. Clark H. Pinnock (Minneapolis: Bethany House, 1975), 168.

the world" results in their no longer belonging to the world, but from now on to him. This is an election to salvation.

In Jesus' great prayer, he speaks of those chosen for salvation as the Father's gift to his Son. His mission is based on their prior election by the Father. So Jesus gives eternal life and reveals the Father to them alone. He prays for them alone, and asks the Father to take them to heaven (17:2, 6, 9–10, 24).

Jesus' Place in the Story. The Bible's story of election began with God's choosing of Abraham, a former idolater, and promising to make him into a nation through his son Isaac. God reaffirmed his promises to Isaac's son Jacob, whose name God changed to "Israel." To the man Israel, God gave twelve sons, who became the fathers of the twelve tribes of the nation of Israel. Although that nation failed to keep covenant with God, he did not give up on humankind but, as he had promised (Isa. 42:1), sent one Israelite—Jesus Christ—to accomplish redemption for the nation and the world. Christ as the true Israel supplanted rebellious Israel in God's plan (though he would still honor his promises to the patriarchs: Rom. 11:26–29). But there is still one more chapter of the story to tell—Christ the true Israelite chooses twelve disciples to replace the twelve tribes and to inaugurate the Christian church.

Scene Two: The Election of the Twelve Disciples

Jesus Chooses Twelve Disciples. Jesus Christ, the prophesied servant of the Lord who embodied Israel in himself, planned to make a new beginning for Israel. After going to a mountain to be alone, he prayed to God all night and in the morning did something that would change the world.

> And when day came, he called his disciples and chose from them twelve, whom he named apostles: Simon, whom he named Peter, and Andrew his brother, and James and John, and Philip, and Bartholomew, and Matthew, and Thomas, and James the son of Alphaeus, and Simon who was called the Zealot, and Judas the

son of James, and Judas Iscariot, who became a traitor. (Luke
6:13–16; cf. Matt. 10:1–4; Mark 3:13–19)

The evangelists in different ways emphasize that Jesus chose
twelve men. Luke indicates (as quoted above) that, from among
a larger number of followers, Jesus handpicked twelve disciples
and named them apostles. Matthew calls them both "his twelve
disciples" and "the twelve apostles" (Matt. 10:1, 2). Mark accen-
tuates the number "twelve" by using it twice without any noun
to modify: "And he appointed twelve," and "He appointed the
twelve" (Mark 3:14, 16).

It is important to note that Jesus' election of the Twelve is a
historical election because Judas Iscariot was included among
them. Unlike the other eleven, Judas Iscariot was only historically elect, not eternally elect. We explored how absolute divine
control and genuine human freedom fit together in chapter 8 on
free will. For now, we note that although Judas was not chosen
for salvation (John 13:10–11, 18), Scripture consistently blames
Judas's fate on his own ungodliness and rebellion (John 12:4–6;
13:21, 26–30; 18:2–5). Every list of the twelve disciples in the
Synoptic Gospels includes the fact that Judas Iscariot was the
betrayer. Although John's gospel does not give a list, in it Jesus
is most blunt: "Did I not choose you, the Twelve? And yet one of
you is a devil" (John 6:70; see also v. 71).

Why did Jesus choose twelve disciples and not seven or
fifteen or twenty? Because he used the number "twelve" symboli-
cally to indicate that he chose twelve men to replace the twelve
tribes of Israel.[2] This explains why the disciples were eager to
replace Judas after he had betrayed Christ and committed suicide. In Acts 1, after listing the eleven disciples by name, Luke
records that Judas had been "numbered among" them "and was
allotted his share in" their ministry (Acts 1:17). He goes on to
say that one of the men who knew Christ during his earthly

2. See William L. Lane, *The Gospel according to Mark* (Grand Rapids: Eerdmans,
1974), 133; I. Howard Marshall, *New Testament Theology* (Downers Grove, IL: InterVarsity
Press, 2004), 158–59.

ministry and saw him after his resurrection "must become with us a witness to his resurrection" (v. 22). They then asked God to show them which of two men, Joseph called Barsabbas or Matthias, he had chosen "to take the place in this ministry and apostleship from which Judas turned aside to go to his own place" (v. 25). "The lot fell on Matthias, and he was numbered with the eleven disciples" (v. 26). Note the inclusion of the word "numbered" in verses 17 and 26, which speak of Judas's being "numbered among us" and Matthias's being "numbered with the eleven," respectively. At the two borders of the passage, Luke draws attention to numbering and then mentions "the eleven" in order to reinforce the symbolism of the twelve apostles' replacing Israel's twelve tribes.

Later in his ministry, Jesus predicts that his disciples will reign over the twelve tribes. His disciples ask Jesus what their lot will be in the world to come in the light of their leaving everything in this world to follow him. Jesus replies, "Truly, I say to you, in the new world, when the Son of Man will sit on his glorious throne, you who have followed me will also sit on twelve thrones, judging the twelve tribes of Israel" (Matt. 19:28; see also Luke 22:30). Jesus' twelve disciples will rule over the twelve tribes of Israel in the world to come. That is, they will reign with Jesus in his coming kingdom, replacing Jacob's twelve sons as leaders of the people of God.

Revelation twice connects the twelve apostles with the twelve tribes. John sees twenty-four thrones around God's throne, "and seated on the thrones were twenty-four elders" (Rev. 4:4). Greg Beale asserts, "The elders are the twelve tribes and the twelve apostles representing the entire community of the redeemed of both testaments."[3] They "fall down before him who is seated on the throne" in worship for creation and "before the Lamb" in worship for redemption (Rev. 4:10; 5:8). Here we see the twelve heads of the tribes and the twelve apostles serving as worship leaders in the future kingdom. The symbolism is powerful: God's people of

---

3. G. K. Beale, *The Book of Revelation: A Commentary on the Greek Text*, New International Greek Testament Commentary (Grand Rapids: Eerdmans, 1999), 323.

both Testaments will worship the Trinity forever. And prominent among them are the twelve tribes and twelve apostles.

At the end of the Bible's story, the New Jerusalem appears. The city of God has twelve gates, "and on the gates the names of the twelve tribes of the sons of Israel were inscribed" (Rev. 21:12). Furthermore, the city's wall had twelve foundations, "and on them were the twelve names of the twelve apostles of the Lamb" (Rev. 21:14). Surely the twelve tribes and twelve apostles occupy important places in the final kingdom of God! John thereby signifies their importance in God's plan. Notice how once again Scripture connects them.

Jesus chooses twelve disciples to "be with him" (Mark 3:14) and then to be apostles, sent by him to preach the gospel. In this way, Jesus indicated that the twelve tribes of Israel had failed in their mission and that he intended through a new twelve to succeed where the nation had failed. He, the true Israel, would create a new Israel through the twelve apostles. How? By commissioning them as witnesses to his resurrection. Through the apostles' proclamation, the New Testament church would be built.

The Apostles Preach the Gospel. The Holy Spirit's coming at Pentecost transformed Jesus' timid followers into bold apostles, who preached fearlessly that Jesus was the Jewish Messiah and risen Lord. At the close of the first Christian sermon, Peter announced: "Let all the house of Israel therefore know for certain that God has made him both Lord and Christ, this Jesus whom you crucified" (Acts 2:36). As the twelve sons of Israel fathered twelve tribes, so Jesus' twelve disciples were to have many spiritual sons and daughters through evangelism.

1. God fulfills his promise to Abraham to bless all nations. Through the apostles' proclamation, God fulfilled his promise to Abraham to bless all nations, as Peter taught in his preaching:

You are the sons of the prophets and of the covenant that God made with your fathers, saying to Abraham, "And in your offspring shall all the families of the earth be blessed." God,

having raised up his servant, sent him to you first, to bless
you by turning every one of you from your wickedness. (Acts
3:25–26, quoting Gen. 22:18)

Peter tells the Jews that God fulfilled the promise of blessing to
Abraham by sending Christ to them first to bless them. Paul,
in Galatians, explains that the ultimate fulfillment involved the
gospel going to the Gentiles also: "And the Scripture, foreseeing
that God would justify the Gentiles by faith, preached the gospel
beforehand to Abraham, saying, 'In you shall all the nations be
blessed'" (Gal. 3:7–8, quoting Gen. 12:3).

The nation of Israel was unsuccessful in its role as God's
instrument of blessing the surrounding nations. But the apostles,
handpicked by Jesus to replace the nation, succeeded where Israel
had failed. Through Paul's ministry especially, scores of Gentiles
came to Christ. For instance, after Paul and Barnabas were reviled
in Pisidian Antioch by jealous Jewish leaders, they turned to the
Gentiles, who gladly received them and the gospel. Paul regarded
this move from Jews to Gentiles as fulfilling Scripture: "I have
made you a light for the Gentiles, that you may bring salvation
to the ends of the earth" (Acts 13:47, quoting Isa. 49:6).

2. The church is the new Israel. A significant component of the
apostles' message was that the church was the new Israel. Peter
describes the Christian church with half a dozen Old Testament
designations for Israel:

> But you are a chosen race, a royal priesthood, a holy nation,
> a people for his own possession, that you may proclaim the
> excellencies of him who called you out of darkness into his
> marvelous light. Once you were not a people, but now you are
> God's people; once you had not received mercy, but now you
> have received mercy. (1 Peter 2:9–10)

Peter's message is unmistakable: in contrast with Old Testament
national Israel, the Christian church is the new, spiritual Israel.

Paul called the church "the Israel of God" (Gal. 6:16) and,
writing to the church in Philippi, defined "the real circumcision"

166

in these terms: "We . . . who worship by the Spirit of God and glory in Christ Jesus and put no confidence in the flesh" (Phil. 3:3).

The writer to the Hebrews also depicts the church in words originally applied by the Old Testament to Israel:

> But you have come to Mount Zion and to the city of the living God, the heavenly Jerusalem, and to innumerable angels in festal gathering, and to the assembly of the firstborn who are enrolled in heaven, and to God, the judge of all, and to the spirits of the righteous made perfect, and to Jesus, the mediator of a new covenant, and to the sprinkled blood that speaks a better word than the blood of Abel. (Heb. 12:22–24)

The writer transforms Mount Zion and Jerusalem into spiritual, heavenly realities as a part of his demonstration that Jesus and the new covenant are superior to the Mosaic covenant. As a result, his readers should cling to Jesus and not turn away from him to escape persecution.

The apostles speak with one voice: the Christian church is the fulfillment of Old Testament Israel. As such, it has supplanted the nation as the spiritual Israel and the people of God.

3. God calls his elect through the gospel. When the apostles preach, they call on people to repent and believe the gospel. Paul summarizes his preaching as "testifying both to Jews and to Greeks of repentance toward God and of faith in our Lord Jesus Christ" (Acts 20:21). Where do the apostles place their confidence of results? Not in their own oratory or persuasion, but in the Spirit's power to convert their hearers (1 Cor. 2:3–5). And not in the ability of their hearers to choose God, because they have none (1 Cor. 2:14; 2 Cor. 4:4). Rather, they put their confidence in the Lord, who works through his Word to bring sinners to himself.

Twice in Acts, readers are permitted to look behind the scenes as the apostles preach. When Paul and Barnabas encounter Jewish opposition in Antioch in Pisidia, they turn to the Gentiles. The Gentiles rejoiced and honored the gospel, "and as many as were appointed to eternal life believed" (Acts 13:48). The apostles' confidence for results in ministry was in the sovereign grace of God. Paul is discouraged in Corinth when Jews abusively oppose him. In response, he begins to preach to Gentiles (Acts 18:7–8). The Lord appears to him in a vision, urging him to continue (v. 9). God assures him, "I have many in this city who are my people" (v. 10). Learning that some Corinthians belonged to God even before they believed gave Paul confidence of results in ministry (v. 11).

The Apostles Teach Election. In addition to preaching, Jesus' apostles wrote the New Testament. In so doing they explored many themes, including election. Their teaching on predestination is the crown of the whole Bible's teaching on the subject.

1. The author of election. The apostles, in every place but one, present God the Father as the author of election. Paul writes: "Blessed be the God and Father of our Lord Jesus Christ, who has blessed us . . . , even as he chose us. . . . In love he predestined us" (Eph. 1:3–5).[4] In one passage (John 15:16, 19), Jesus indicates that he, too, is the author of election, as previously argued.[5] Of course, since the three persons of the Trinity are to be distinguished but never separated, it is best to say that the Trinity chose us for salvation, especially the Father and in one place the Son.

2. The objects of election. Arminians err by teaching corporate election and downplaying individual election, while Calvinists commit the opposite error—teaching individual election and downplaying corporate election. The apostles teach both. Tracing the pronouns through the passage in Ephesians 1 shows that the same people who were chosen ("us," v. 4) and predestined ("us," v. 5) also "were the first to hope in Christ" ("we," v. 12). Individuals "hope in Christ," that is, trust him for salvation. But individuals make up churches, such as "the saints who are in Ephesus," to whom Paul addresses Ephesians (v. 1). God chose individuals to constitute the Christian church.

4. Other passages include Rom. 8:29–30; 2 Thess. 2:13; 2 Tim. 1:9.
5. See pages 66–67, 161–62.

3. The time of election. Only when the Bible's story line reaches the apostles do we learn that God's election took place before creation. Three Scriptures reveal this truth, and they overlap in saying that God chose us for final sanctification "before the foundation of the world"; he gave us saving grace "before the ages began"; and people's names were written "in the book of life from the foundation of the world" (Eph. 1:4; 2 Tim. 1:9; Rev. 17:8). What is the significance of the time of predestination? God indicates that election is all his doing; we had nothing to do with it, for we did not even exist before creation.[6]

4. The basis of election. The apostles most clearly in Scripture reveal the basis for election, both negatively and positively. Negatively, Paul teaches that election is not based on anything human beings do or will: "So then it depends not on human will or exertion, but on God, who has mercy" (Rom. 9:16). Positively, election is based on God's compassion and will. In many ways Scripture expresses the fact that predestination is based on God's compassion: his love beforehand (Rom. 8:29), his mercy (Rom. 9:15, 16, 18), his love (Eph. 1:4–5), his grace (Rom. 11:5; 2 Tim. 1:9). Many other times Scripture teaches that predestination is based on God's sovereign will: God's purpose (Rom. 9:11; Eph. 1:5, 11; 2 Tim. 1:9), his prerogative (Rom. 9:15, 16, 18), his will (Eph. 1:9, 11).

It is best to combine the two aspects: the basis of election is God's compassionate will, his sovereign mercy, his good pleasure. Paul says it succinctly: "God . . . saved us and called us to a holy calling, not because of our works but because of *his own purpose and grace*" (2 Tim. 1:8–9).

5. Election "in Christ." When Paul twice speaks of God's choosing us "in him" (Eph. 1:4, 11), he refers to union with Christ. In these places, Paul says that God chose people before

6. The meaning is similar to Paul's saying: "Though they [Jacob and Esau] were not yet born and had done nothing either good or bad—in order that God's purpose of election might continue, not because of works but because of his call—she [Rebecca] was told, 'The older will serve the younger'" (Rom. 9:11–12). Paul states the reason why God spoke to Rebecca, their mother, before Jacob and Esau were born: "in order that God's purpose of election might continue."

the foundation of the world (v. 4). In every other case when Paul uses the phrase "in Christ," except for 2 Timothy 1:9, he tells of God's uniting people to Christ *in history*. God's choosing us "in him before the foundation of the world" (Eph. 1:4; see also v. 11) speaks of our union with Christ before creation. But because we did not exist before our creation, Paul speaks of God's plan to unite us to Christ.

Though Arminianism holds that election "in Christ" means that God chose people for salvation based on his foreknowledge of their faith in Christ, Paul does not speak of a condition that sinners must meet in order for God to choose them. Paul's words do not speak of human beings' response, but of God's sovereign will. It is the same in Ephesians 1:11, where Paul says, "In him we have obtained an inheritance, having been predestined according to the purpose of him who works all things according to the counsel of his will." The apostle teaches that God not only chose a people for himself, but also chose the means by which he would actually save that people—he would send his Son and Spirit and unite them to Christ in saving grace.

6. Election considered within God's plan. The apostles John and Paul place election within the larger picture of God's plan of salvation. In John 6, Jesus speaks of the Father's giving of people to Jesus (a picture of election, v. 37), the Father's drawing of them to him (v. 44), their coming to him (a picture of faith, vv. 35, 37, 40, 44, 45), his preserving them in salvation (vv. 37, 39), and his raising them on the last day (vv. 39, 40, 44). In this way, Jesus places predestination first in a chain of predestination, drawing or calling, faith in him, preservation, and resurrection to salvation.

With different pictures but overlapping ideas, Paul locates predestination in the plan of salvation in Romans 8: "For those whom he foreknew he also predestined to be conformed to the image of his Son. . . . And those whom he predestined he also called, and those whom he called he also justified, and those whom he justified he also glorified" (vv. 29–30). Paul's pattern is foreknowledge (God's loving his people in advance), predestination (his choosing them), calling (his summoning them to

Christ), justification (his declaring them righteous in Christ), and glorification (his causing them to partake of Christ's glory).

Both John and Paul, then, see election or predestination as one of God's works among many performed on behalf of God's people to save them from beginning (election) to end (resurrection and glorification). Truly God is good to sinners!

Is Israel still elect? God's Old Testament people Israel, in general, rejected their Messiah. Paul says that this spiritual hardening is "partial." It will last until the conversion of all the Gentiles. "And in this way all Israel will be saved" (Rom. 11:26). Although some have taken "Israel" here to mean spiritual Israel—the church—in the other ten instances where the term occurs in Romans 9–11, it signifies the Jews over against the Gentiles. "Israel" in Romans 11:26 also refers to ethnic Israel, the physical descendants of Abraham. Paul means that God will save the sum total of Israelites who believe in Christ between his first and second comings, with a big conversion near Christ's second coming.

Romans 11:28 reinforces this conclusion: "As regards the gospel, they are enemies of God for your sake. But as regards election, they are beloved for the sake of their forefathers." Because the Jews reject the gospel, they are God's enemies; but they are loved by God because of his election of the patriarchs. Paul continues: "For the gifts and the calling of God are irrevocable" (v. 29). God will not renege on his Old Testament promises to the Jews. Since the coming of Christ, however, no one, including Jews, will ever be saved apart from faith in him. All who possess that faith become a part of the one Christian church, made up of believing Jews and Gentiles.

7. *Historical and eternal election.* The Bible justifies John Frame's distinction between historical and eternal election.[7] The former refers to the election of the nation of Israel in the Old Testament and that of the church in the New Testament. God chooses these corporate entities, although some Old Testament Jews and New Testament church members are unsaved. Those

---

7. John Frame, *The Doctrine of God* (Phillipsburg, NJ: P&R Publishing, 2002), 317–30.

eternally elect, by contrast, are chosen by God for salvation, in addition to being historically elect. Judas Iscariot is an example of a New Testament figure who is historically elect but not eternally elect.

8. *Double predestination.* Although Scripture's major thrust concerning election is God's eternal election of his people for salvation, the Bible also teaches that God is the Lord of every human being's destiny. Jesus distinguishes between (a) those who "do not believe because" they "are not part of" his "flock" and (b) his "sheep," to whom he gives "eternal life" (John 10:26–28). Along with "vessels of mercy, which he has prepared beforehand for glory," there are "vessels of wrath prepared for destruction" (Rom. 9:22–23). Paul divides first-century Israel into "the elect," who obtained salvation, and "the rest," who were hardened (Rom. 11:7). Peter speaks of unbelievers' stumbling over Christ "because they disobey the word, as they were destined to do" (1 Peter 2:8).

Scripture teaches that although all human beings deserve God's eternal displeasure because of Adam's and their own sin, God in mercy chose multitudes for salvation. In so doing, for reasons hidden in his own mind, he passed over many others, allowing them to pay the penalty for their sins.

9. *The goals of election.* God's eternal election points toward the future. Its goals are varied. As regards the creation, the goal is cosmic restoration—"to unite all things in him, things in heaven and things on earth" (Eph. 1:10). For his people, the goal is final salvation expressed in many ways: holiness (Eph. 1:4), adoption (Eph. 1:5), conformity to Christ (Rom. 8:29), and glory (Rom. 8:30; 2 Thess. 2:14). As pertains to God himself, the goal of predestination is his own glory (Eph. 1:6, 12). Paul sums up matters well: "In him we have obtained an inheritance, having been predestined according to the purpose of him who works all things according to the counsel of his will, so that we who were the first to hope in Christ might be to the praise of his glory" (Eph. 1:11–12).

Objections to and
Applications of Election

After discussing a dozen New Testament passages that speak of God's choosing people for salvation, Paul Jewett scolds:

> Few, indeed, are those who today speak as these Scriptures do, so far have we drifted from the biblical moorings of our faith regarding the doctrine of election. But in New Testament times it was not so. Even when they did not use the word "election" (ἐκλογή), it was natural for the early Christians to speak of God as the electing God.[1]

This book has sought to reestablish "the biblical moorings of our faith regarding the doctrine of election." Toward that end it has traced the doctrine of "the electing God" through the Bible and summarized it—the end of the previous chapter serves as a virtual systematic summary of predestination. Two important matters remain: to treat objections to the Reformed view of election and to point to the Bible's applications of election.

Our Response to Election

Scripture not only teaches election but also applies it to life. We will consider objections to predestination while we examine six scriptural applications of it.[2]

---

1. Paul K. Jewett, *Election and Predestination* (Grand Rapids: Eerdmans, 1985), 25.
2. John Calvin answered many of these objections in *Institutes* 3.23 and in *The Eternal Predestination of God.*

- Praise
- Thanksgiving and Humility
- Incentive for Evangelism
- Perseverance and Service
- Confidence in God
- Assurance of God's Love and Care

Praise

Election is sometimes labeled as unfair and arbitrary.[3] Referring to the Calvinist portrayal of God, Terry L. Miethe writes:

> Certainly, this "God" would either be (1) grossly unfair because he chose "before the foundation of the world" some to be saved and some to be damned, therefore never really giving anyone a chance, or (2) a respecter of persons because he chose some and not others, or at least very arbitrary in his choosing. . . . The "god" spoken of above surely would not be worthy of worship and certainly would not be the Christian God.[4]

The Bible, however, never accuses God of unfairness in election; instead, one scriptural application of predestination is to foster God's praise:

> Blessed be the God and Father of our Lord Jesus Christ, who has blessed us in Christ with every spiritual blessing in the heavenly places, even as he chose us in him before the foundation of the world, that we should be holy and blameless before him. In love he predestined us for adoption through Jesus Christ, according to the purpose of his will, to the praise of his glorious grace. (Eph. 1:3–6)

Although we do not understand everything about the Father's choosing of us, he has told us all we need to know. And his

---

3. We addressed the charge that God is arbitrary in election on pages 49–50.

4. Terry L. Miethe, "The Universal Power of the Atonement," in *The Grace of God, the Will of Man*, ed. Clark H. Pinnock (Grand Rapids: Zondervan, 1989), 81–82.

election of a people in Christ is cause for adoring the Father, as Augustine said: "God's grace is not given according to the deserts of the recipients, but according to the good pleasure of His will, to the praise and glory of His own grace; so that he who glorieth may by no means glory in himself, but in the Lord."[5]

Thanksgiving and Humility

Election is sometimes said to foster elitism; "the elect" might consider themselves superior to others and be prideful. William Klein explains: "Election embarrasses some Christians. They are reluctant to say, 'God chose me,' when he apparently passed by others. Such a claim makes them uncomfortable; it seems so arrogant, so exclusive."[6]

Scripture never conveys such an attitude; instead, God's predestination engenders gratitude. "But we ought always to give thanks to God for you, brothers beloved by the Lord, because God chose you as the firstfruits to be saved, through sanctification by the Spirit and belief in the truth," Paul wrote to the Thessalonians (2 Thess. 2:13). Do you thank God that he chose people for salvation, including you, if you trust Christ as your Lord and Savior?

Augustine spoke of thanksgiving for God's preceding love in memorable fashion:

Wherefore if I am unwilling to appear ungrateful to men who have loved me, because some advantage of my labour has attained to them before they loved me, how much rather am I unwilling to be ungrateful to God, whom we should not love unless He had first loved us and made us to love Him![7]

Scripture does not teach that election engenders pride, but just the opposite. God puts us in our place when he declares

5. Augustine, *On the Gift of Perseverance* 28, in *Nicene and Post-Nicene Fathers*, ed. Philip Schaff, vol. 5 1st ser. (repr. Grand Rapids: Eerdmans, 1971), 536.
6. William W. Klein, *The New Chosen People* (Grand Rapids: Academie Books, 1990), 19.
7. Augustine, *On the Gift of Perseverance* 56, 548.

concerning salvation: "So then it depends not on human will or exertion, but on God, who has mercy" (Rom. 9:16). What place is left for pride when Scripture says of God: "So then he has mercy on whomever he wills, and he hardens whomever he wills" (v. 18)? And Paul further demolishes our pride: "But who are you, O man, to answer back to God? Will what is molded say to its molder, 'Why have you made me like this?' Has the potter no right over the clay, to make out of the same lump one vessel for honored use and another for dishonorable use?" (vv. 20–21). A "proud Calvinist" is an oxymoron, a contradiction in terms—but, unfortunately, there are many. God calls all Christians to ongoing repentance and humility.

Incentive for Evangelism

Some have frowned on the Calvinistic view of election as discouraging evangelism. "Calvinists can't make coherent sense of their claim that God makes a bona fide offer of salvation to persons he has not elected for salvation, nor can they explain how God can truly have compassion for such persons."[8] But in the Scriptures, God's choice of a people for salvation stimulates evangelism.[9] After Paul and Barnabas, on the first missionary journey, were reviled by jealous Jewish leaders in Antioch of Pisidia, they brought the gospel to Gentiles. The Gentiles rejoiced, "and as many as were appointed to eternal life believed" (Acts 13:48). Here, rather than hindering the apostles' evangelistic efforts, God's sovereign predestination made them successful.

We see a similar scenario when Paul meets opposition on the second missionary journey at Corinth. The Lord says to him in a vision: "Do not be afraid, but go on speaking and do not be silent, for I am with you, and no one will attack you to harm you, for I have many in this city who are my people" (Acts 18:9–10).

---

8. Jerry L. Walls and Joseph R. Dongell, *Why I Am Not a Calvinist* (Downers Grove, IL: InterVarsity Press, 2004), 188. The point is developed on pp. 188–94.
9. An outstanding resource is J. I. Packer's *Evangelism and the Sovereignty of God* (Downers Grove, IL: InterVarsity Press, 1973).

Far from discouraging evangelism, God's election spurs Paul on to greater witness for Christ.

Charles Haddon Spurgeon, the famous nineteenth-century Baptist preacher, when asked why he preached if only some persons are elected, replied:

> That is why we preach! If there are so many fish to be taken in the net, I will go and catch some of them. Because many are ordained to be caught, I spread my nets with eager expectation. I never could see why that should repress our zealous efforts. It seems to me to be the very thing that should awaken us with energy—that God has a people, and that these people shall be brought in.[10]

Perseverance and Service

A common objection to election is that it destroys motivation and promotes laziness. "Such a notion, indistinguishable from fatalism, is inconsistent with human freedom and undermines the reality of history and man's moral responsibility."[11] If God is in control, this line of reasoning goes, what difference does it make whether we pray or evangelize or not? The Bible teaches that God is in control over all things, including the destinies of human beings.[12] But it also teaches that God, our covenant Lord, regards the actions of us, his covenant partners, as significant. In fact, Scripture uses divine sovereignty to stimulate fruitful service for God. We saw this in Acts 18:9–10, where God told Paul that he had many of his people in Corinth to encourage Paul to keep preaching.

We see it also when Paul writes from prison:

> Remember Jesus Christ, risen from the dead, the offspring of David, as preached in my gospel, for which I am suffering,

10. Charles Haddon Spurgeon, *Metropolitan Tabernacle Pulpit*, 63 vols. (Pasadena, TX: Pilgrim Publications, 1981), 26:622.
11. Clark H. Pinnock, ed., *Grace Unlimited* (Minneapolis: Bethany House, 1975), 17. For the differences between predestination and fatalism, see this book, pages 148–49.
12. See pages 143–44 for God's control over all and 103–24 for his control over human beings' destinies.

bound with chains as a criminal. But the word of God is not bound! Therefore I endure everything for the sake of the elect, that they also may obtain the salvation that is in Christ Jesus with eternal glory. (2 Tim. 2:8–10)

Paul, who preaches that Christ is divine and human, is imprisoned, but God's Word cannot be! Because of that powerful Word, Paul endures many sufferings "for the sake of the elect." Paul regards certain people as elect, as chosen by God for salvation. He suffers for their sake. Why? "That they also may obtain the salvation that is in Christ Jesus with eternal glory" (v. 10). Paul does not regard God's election of people as stifling his service for Christ. Instead, God's sovereignty in salvation motivates Paul to get the gospel to those chosen, that they might believe and be rescued.

John Calvin takes to task those who use election as an excuse for sin and sloth:

> They say they go on unconcerned in their vices; for if they are of the number of the elect, vices will not hinder them from being at last brought into life. Yet Paul teaches that we have been chosen to this end: that we may lead a holy and blameless life [Eph. 1:4]. If election has as its goal holiness of life, it ought rather to arouse and goad us eagerly to set our mind upon it than to serve as a pretext for doing nothing. What a great difference there is between these two things: to cease well-doing because election is sufficient for salvation, and to devote ourselves to the pursuit of good as the appointed goal of election![13]

Confidence in God

Calvinistic election is sometimes accused of being defeatist and of squelching hope, as Clark Pinnock claims: "There is no predestination to salvation or damnation in the Bible. . . . It is a pity that a doctrine intended to communicate hope has been

13. John Calvin, *Institutes of the Christian Religion* 3.23.12, ed. John T. McNeill (Philadelphia: Westminster Press, 1960), 960.

turned into such a fearful concept."[14] To the contrary, Scripture uses the doctrine to spawn hope for the future. Paul points the suffering Roman believers to future glory made certain by God's sovereign plan:

> For those whom he foreknew he also predestined to be conformed to the image of his Son, in order that he might be the firstborn among many brothers. And those whom he predestined he also called, and those whom he called he also justified, and those whom he justified he also glorified. (Rom. 8:29–30)

The prospect of final conformity to Christ and future glorification, both of which result from God's foreloving and predestinating his people, encourages believers to be optimistic about the future. Biblically, then, election does not stifle hope but fans it.

Calvin extols the doctrine of election as a means whereby God gives confidence to his people:

> To make it clear that our salvation comes about solely from God's mere generosity—we must be called back to the course of election. . . .
>
> And, as Christ teaches, here is our only ground for firmness and confidence; in order to free us of all fear and render us victorious amid so many dangers, snares, and mortal struggles, he promises that whatever the Father has entrusted into his keeping will be safe [John 10:28–29].[15]

Assurance of God's Love and Care

"Calvinist believers who struggle with their assurance can never know with certainty that they are one of the elect," state Jerry Walls and Joseph Dongell.[16] This objection, it is claimed, causes Calvinists to lack assurance of their salvation. The oppo-

---

14. Pinnock, *Grace Unlimited*, 18.
15. Calvin, *Institutes* 3.23.12, 921–22.
16. Walls and Dongell, *Why I Am Not a Calvinist*, 198–203. See also William J. Abraham, "Predestination and Assurance," in *The Grace of God, the Will of Man*, ed. Clark H. Pinnock (Grand Rapids: Zondervan, 1989), 235.

site is true biblically: God's strong arm is the foundation for our assurance of God's love and care. Jesus assures his sheep:

> My sheep hear my voice, and I know them, and they follow me. I give them eternal life, and they will never perish, and no one will snatch them out of my hand. My Father, who has given them to me, is greater than all, and no one is able to snatch them out of the Father's hand. (John 10:27–29)

As we saw earlier, one of John's themes of election is the antecedent identity of the sheep, prior to their believing in Jesus.[17] The sheep, marked out beforehand for salvation, believe. To them Jesus gives eternal life and promises that they will never be lost again because the Father and he will keep them safe. Election assures believers of God's love, as Spurgeon teaches:

> For I am persuaded that the doctrine of predestination—the blessed truth of providence—is one of the softest pillows upon which the Christian can lay his head, and one of the strongest staffs upon which he may lean in his pilgrimage along this rough road. Cheer up, Christian! Things are not left to chance: no blind fate rules the world. God hath purposes, and those purposes are fulfilled. God hath plans, and those plans are wise, and never can be dislocated. Oh trust in him and thou shalt have each fruit in its season, the mercy in its time, the trial in its period, and the deliverance in its needed moment.[18]

How do the elect know their election? Does predestination encourage speculation, as is sometimes claimed? It all depends on where we look for our knowledge of our election, as Calvin cautions:

> For just as those engulf themselves in a deadly abyss who, to make their election more certain, investigate God's eternal plan

17. See pages 63–64.
18. Charles Haddon Spurgeon, *New Park Street Pulpit*, 6 vols. (Pasadena, TX: Pilgrim Publications, 1981), 6:455.

apart from his Word, so those who rightly and duly examine it as it is contained in his Word reap the inestimable fruit of comfort. Let this, therefore, be the way of our inquiry: to begin with God's call and to end with it.[19]

Calvin is correct; we know our election when God effectively calls us to faith in his Son. "For we know, brothers loved by God, that he has chosen you, because our gospel came to you not only in word, but also in power and in the Holy Spirit and with full conviction" (1 Thess. 1:4–5). The Lord never instructs us to probe into his eternal counsels to learn of our election; instead, he points us to the gospel. When people trust Christ as Lord and Savior, they know that God has chosen them. Calvin aptly writes: "But if we have been chosen in him, we shall not find assurance of our election in ourselves; and not even in God the Father, if we conceive of him as severed from his Son. Christ, then, is the mirror wherein we must, and without self-deception may, contemplate our own election."[20]

Conclusion

It is not enough to know what the Bible teaches. We must also know *why* it teaches what it teaches and then act on that teaching. This is to be concerned about the function of Scripture—the purposes for which God gave us his Word. This chapter has surveyed some of the most important purposes for which God revealed the doctrine of election. In spite of the common objections, Scripture teaches predestination and does so for good reasons: that his people might praise and humbly thank him, that they might be motivated to spread the good news, persevere, and serve him, and that they might have great confidence in their God, and enjoy his love and care for them.

19. Calvin, *Institutes* 3.24.4, 969.
20. Ibid., 3.24.5, 970.

For all these reasons, election pertains to life in the twenty-first century as much as to that in the first century. This book thus comes full circle, for it began by exploring some insecurities of contemporary life and suggesting that the Bible's teaching on predestination might offer help. We can now see that this is in fact the case. Because contemporary life is characterized by much insecurity in a variety of spheres, it is good for us to hear God's comforting and confidence-building message of election.

For example, the teaching that God powerfully works all things for the good of his people (Rom. 8:28) offers hope for the future for those experiencing family dysfunction. Such knowledge is not a magic wand that will make our family problems disappear, but it can help us tackle those problems with a quiet confidence that God cares and will continue to work for his glory and our good. "He who began a good work in you will bring it to completion at the day of Jesus Christ" (Phil. 1:6).

The fact that God has chosen individuals to belong to him and to one another in the church can help us overcome the loneliness brought on by an abuse of technology. It can motivate us to discipline our use of technological aids and toys in order to make time for the family of God—the people, including us, whom our heavenly Father in love chose to adopt (Eph. 1:5).

Our fears of terrorism may never be completely quieted, but the fact that "the LORD has established his throne in the heavens, and his kingdom rules over all" (Ps. 103:19) helps us to rest in him. He does not want us to live paralyzed by fears of the unknown but instead to draw near to the One we know, the Lord God Almighty, who holds the world and us in his strong and gentle arms. Although we know terrors on earth that Jonathan Edwards never dreamed of, if we approach God in the same manner that he did, we will have peace of mind to face whatever comes our way: "God's absolute sovereignty . . . is what my mind seems to rest assured of. . . . The doctrine has very often appeared exceeding pleasant, bright, and sweet. Absolute sovereignty is what I love to ascribe to God. . . . It has often been my delight to approach God, and adore him as a sovereign God."[21]

Moreover, biblical teaching on election exposes the West's notion of radical autonomy for the sham that it is. We do not have to live enslaved to the myths that we must keep reinventing ourselves to be free and that our greatest goal is to buy more and greater things. These are lies of a false freedom—lies that we must reject. We need to live with a growing awareness that true freedom is knowing, loving, serving, and enjoying the living God, to whom belongs eternal praise for choosing us and making himself our God and us his own people.

More than 170 years ago, Josiah Conder wrote of that freedom in a hymn:

'Tis not that I did choose thee, for, Lord, that could not be;
This heart would still refuse thee, hadst thou not chosen me.
Thou from the sin that stained me hast cleansed and set me
        free;
Of old thou hast ordained me, that I should live to thee.

'Twas sov'reign mercy called me and taught my op'ning mind;
The world had else enthralled me, to heav'nly glories blind.
My heart owns none before thee, for thy rich grace I thirst;
This knowing, if I love thee, thou must have loved me first.

Josiah Conder, 1836

---

21. Quoted in John Piper, *The Supremacy of God in Preaching* (Grand Rapids: Baker, 1990), 76–77.

Questions for Study and Reflection

Chapter 1—Why a Book on Election and Free Will?

1. Tell why you think Christians sometimes discuss election (predestination) unkindly with other Christians.

2. Explain why it is important for Christians to disagree in love for the sake of the unity of the church and for the sake of our witness to the world.

3. Were you aware that the Bible speaks of God's election of Israel, Christ, and the church? What questions does this fact raise in your mind?

4. Why does Scripture have so many passages on divine election?

5. What examples of the insecurity of contemporary life resonate with you?

6. Can you see ways that the Bible's message about God's control of all things, including salvation, can help people struggling with uncertainty?

Chapter 2—Election and Free Will in Church History

1. How does it help to know that Calvinism and Arminianism were around long before John Calvin or James Arminius?

2. Tell why some of Pelagius's views deserved condemnation.

3. How does studying the background of the Synod of Dort help us to understand Arminianism and Calvinism?

4. Why did godly John Wesley so strongly oppose the Calvinist view of election?

5. Spurgeon opposed the "Hyperists." Have you encountered such hyper-Calvinists? Why do you think some today tend toward hyper-Calvinism?

6. Explain how a study of church history demonstrates the need to study what the Bible teaches about election.

Chapter 3—Election in the Old Testament

1. Why do you think God chooses both individuals and the nation of Israel?

2. Explain how Abraham's case shows God's unconditional election of an individual to salvation.

3. Why did God choose Israel alone out of all the nations of the earth?

4. Does the distinction between historical election and eternal election make sense to you? Explain.

5. Tell some of the consequences of God's choice of Israel.

6. Where does the Messiah fit in the Bible's story of election?

Chapter 4—Election in the Gospels and Acts

1. What is the significance of the fact that Jesus includes Gentiles when he speaks about election in Mark 13?

2. Tell how Jesus' own election by God is the same as ours and how it is different.

3. What is the significance of John's teaching that faith is the result of God's election (6:37; 10:27; 17:6)?

4. Do you agree with the author that Jesus is presented as the author of election in John 15:14, 19? If so, what difference does it make?

5. Show that election in John's gospel is for the purposes of salvation and service.

6. How does Acts demonstrate that election strengthens evangelism?

Chapter 5—Election in the General Epistles and Revelation

1. Explain how James 2:5 teaches that God chose people for salvation.

2. What is one way that believers are to make their "calling and election sure" according to 2 Peter 1?

3. What is the significance of the teaching of 1 Peter 2:9; 5:13; and 2 John 1, 13 that God chose the church corporately for salvation?

4. Why does Peter inform us that Christ was chosen to be our Redeemer (1:20; 2:4, 6)?

5. How does Revelation's description of the book of life show election for salvation?

6. What is Revelation's main point in talking about the book of life?

Chapter 6—Election in Paul's Epistles, Part 1

1. How does Romans 11:7 illustrate the distinction between historical election and eternal election?

2. Explain Paul's connection between election and eternal security in Romans 8:33.

3. On what basis does God choose people for salvation (2 Tim. 1:8–9)?

4. What does Paul mean when he teaches that election is "in Christ Jesus" (2 Tim. 1:9)?

5. According to 1 Thessalonians 1:4-5, how do we know that people are elect?

6. What practical benefits does the doctrine of election bring?

Chapter 7—Election in Paul's Epistles, Part 2

1. Show that Ephesians 1:4–5 teaches election unto salvation.

2. How does Romans 9 portray election as individual and not merely corporate?

3. Explain how Romans 9:16 contradicts the idea that election is based on foreseen faith.

4. On what is election based, according to Ephesians 1:4–6, 11? According to Romans 9:13–24?

5. How can election help embattled believers, such as those in first-century Rome?

6. Show how Paul connects election with assurance of final salvation in Romans 8:28–39.

Chapter 8—Free Will

1. What is the significance of the distinction between freedom of choice and true freedom?

2. Tell how true freedom was lost and freedom of choice retained after the fall of Genesis 3.

3. Tell how all of the following are reasons why we are saved: faith, the Spirit's work in hearts, Jesus' death and resurrection, and election.

4. Does God's election before creation undermine our faith in Christ? Explain.

5. What do you make of the fact that the same biblical passages affirm God's sovereignty and our responsibility?

6. What do hyper-Calvinism and Arminianism ironically have in common?

Chapter 9—The Bible's Story of Election

1. Trace the Bible's story of election from Abraham to the nation of Israel.

2. What dramatic event moves the Bible's story from the Old Testament to the New?

3. How does Jesus the Messiah, the chosen servant of the Lord, fulfill the Abrahamic covenant and annul the Mosaic covenant?

4. Tell how Jesus chooses twelve disciples to replace the failed twelve tribes of Israel.

5. What is the apostles' point in teaching that election was before creation (Eph. 1:4; 2 Tim. 1:9; Rev. 17:8)?

6. According to the apostles, what are God's goals for election?

Chapter 10—Objections to and Applications of Election

1. Why does Scripture never label election as unfair, but rather says it is the cause of praise being offered to God?

2. Explain how the Bible's teaching on election humbles us.

3. Do you agree with Spurgeon when he regards election as a stimulus, rather than a hindrance, to evangelism?

4. How does election spark hope in the hearts of God's people?

5. Tell how Scripture uses election to assure believers of salvation.

6. In what practical ways does the Bible's teaching on election pertain to life today?

Select Resources on Election

Arminian Sources

Arminius, James. "A Declaration of the Sentiments of Arminius." In *The Writings of James Arminius*, edited by J. Nichols and W. R. Bagnall, 1:193–275. 3 vols. Reprint, Grand Rapids: Baker, 1956.

Basinger, David, and Randall Basinger, eds. *Predestination & Free Will: Four Views of Divine Sovereignty and Human Freedom*. Downers Grove, IL: InterVarsity Press, 1986.

Forster, Roger T., and V. Paul Marston. *God's Strategy in Human History*. Wheaton, IL: Tyndale House, 1973.

Geisler, Norman. *Chosen but Free: A Balanced View of Divine Election*. 2nd ed. Minneapolis: Bethany House, 2001.

Klein, William W. *The New Chosen People: A Corporate View of Election*. Grand Rapids: Zondervan, 1990.

Marshall, I. Howard. *Kept by the Power of God: A Study of Perseverance and Falling Away*. Minneapolis: Bethany House, 1969.

Oden, Thomas C. *John Wesley's Scriptural Christianity*. Grand Rapids: Zondervan, 1994.

Pinnock, Clark H., ed. *Grace Unlimited*. Minneapolis, MN: Bethany House, 1975.

———, ed. *The Grace of God, the Will of Man: A Case for Arminianism*. Grand Rapids: Zondervan, 1989.

Shank, Robert. *Elect in the Son: A Study of the Doctrine of Election*. Springfield, MO: Westcott Publishers, 1970.

Walls, Jerry L., and Joseph R. Dongell. *Why I Am Not a Calvinist*. Downers Grove, IL: InterVarsity Press, 2004.

Wesley, John. "Predestination Calmly Considered" and "A Dialogue Between a Predestinarian and His Friend." In *The Works of John Wesley*, 10:204–59, 259–66. 14 vols. Reprint, Grand Rapids: Zondervan, 1958.

Calvinist Sources

Augustine. "On the Predestination of the Saints." In *Nicene and Post-Nicene Fathers*,. edited by Philip Schaff. Vol. 5, *Saint Augustine: Anti-Pelagian Writings*, 493–519. Reprint, Grand Rapids: Eerdmans, 1987.

Calvin, John. *Concerning the Eternal Predestination of God*. Translated by J. K. S. Reid. London: James Clarke, 1961.

———. *Institutes of the Christian Religion* 3.21–24. Edited by John T. McNeill. Philadelphia: Westminster Press, 1960.

Carson, Donald. *The Difficult Doctrine of the Love of God*. Wheaton, IL: Crossway, 2000.

———. *Divine Sovereignty and Human Responsibility: Biblical Perspectives in Tension*. Grand Rapids: Baker, 1994.

———. *How Long, O Lord? Reflections on Suffering and Evil*. Grand Rapids: Baker, 1990.

Jewett, Paul. *Election and Predestination*. Grand Rapids: Eerdmans, 1985.

Klooster, Fred. *Calvin's Doctrine of Predestination*. Grand Rapids: Baker, 1977.

Peterson, Robert A., and Michael D. Williams. *Why I Am Not an Arminian*. Downers Grove, IL: InterVarsity Press, 2004.

Piper, John. *The Justification of God: An Exegetical and Theological Study of Romans 9:1–23*. Grand Rapids: Baker, 1983.

Schreiner, Thomas R., and Bruce A. Ware, eds. *Still Sovereign: Contemporary Perspectives on Election, Foreknowledge, and Grace*. Grand Rapids: Baker, 2000.

Sproul, R. C. *Chosen by God*. Wheaton, IL: Tyndale House, 1986.

Venema, Cornelis P. *Heinrich Bullinger and the Doctrine of Predestination*. Grand Rapids: Baker, 2002.

White, James R. *The Potter's Freedom: A Defense of the Reformation and a Rebuttal of Norman Geisler's* Chosen but Free. Amityville, NY: Calvary Press, 2000.

Index of Scripture

196

Index of Subjects and Names